The Backpack Study Series

Backpack Study Secrets
Backpack Speed-Reading Secrets
Backpack Term Paper Secrets
Backpack Test-Taking Secrets

Term
Paper
Secrets

Term Paper Secrets

Research faster, write better, and get great grades

Steven Frank

Adams Media Corporation
HOLBROOK, MASSACHUSETTS

Published by
Adams Media Corporation
260 Center Street, Holbrook, MA 02343

ISBN: 1-58062-026-4

Printed in Canada.

J I H G F E D C B

Library of Congress Cataloging-in-Publication Data
Frank, Steven.
Term paper secrets / Steven Frank.
p.   cm. — (Backpack study series)
ISBN 1-58062-026-4
1. Report writing. I. Title. II. Series.
LB1047.3.F73   1998
371.3'028'1— dc21   98-6273
                                        CIP

This publication is designed to provide accurate and authoritative information with regard
to the subject matter covered. It is sold with the understanding that the publisher is not
engaged in rendering legal, accounting, or other professional advice. If legal advice or
other expert assistance is required, the services of a competent professional person should
be sought.
— From a *Declaration of Principles* jointly adopted by a Committee of the American
Bar Association and a Committee of Publishers and Associations

This book is available at quantity discounts for bulk purchases.
For information, call 1-800-872-5627 (in Massachusetts, 781-767-8100).

Visit our home page at http://www.adamsmedia.com

Contents

10. Editing, Proofreading, and Preparing the Final Paper

Introduction:
Why Write?

In recent years, writing has become more and more an emphasized part of the curriculum at both the high school and college levels. You might be wondering why that should be the case. Why are you being asked to write essays for exams, write papers for your courses, and write so often in classes, even for non-literature courses? What does writing have to do with your education?

Although you may not realize it now, writing is not a meaningless exercise meant to torture you with learning correct grammar and spelling. When you are working on your writing, you're also developing skills that apply to other crucial areas. You're learning, for example, how to generate ideas and convey them in a logical, clear fashion that someone else can appreciate.

In essence, writing is about communication. First you've got to learn what it is you think and want to say. Then you communicate your ideas to others in a way that is accessible and understandable. You can imagine how good communication skills will help you in many other areas — from job interviews to working with colleagues to making friends and dating.

Communication is the key to good, effective essays and term papers. Communication and good ideas. If you ask most instructors what is exceptional about the papers they give top grades, they won't tell you it's perfect spelling, detailed research, or faultless grammar, although all are parts of a well-written paper. What they'll say is important about an essay is the quality of the ideas that the student expresses in it.

Do not underestimate the importance of the ideas you put into your paper. A paper can be beautifully written and carefully researched, yet without interesting ideas, it will be empty, unimpressive, and boring. The kind of paper that impresses is one that packs a punch, one that is provocative, sophisticated, and original. To write this kind of paper, you need to center it upon a powerful argument, one that is distinctly your own. Without one, your paper will not differ from an encyclopedia entry or a chapter in a textbook — just a bunch of facts strung together.

That does not mean, however, that writing style and research are not important. If you cannot express your ideas so that your reader can understand them, they will not amount to much. Always remember: Your reader can't see inside your head; it's up to you to get your ideas out on paper and to present them in a way that your reader can understand and appreciate. Equally important is the research you conduct in the process of writing your paper. You need research to support your claims and to prove that you are an expert in your subject area.

Most writing assignments you get from teachers for classes are not meant to be meaningless writing exercises in which you spit out things you learned in class or cram in as much research as possible to impress your instructor. Rather, they are an opportunity to demonstrate your mastery of the subject. In writing your paper, your goal should be no less than to become an expert on your chosen topic, with something significant and intelligent to say.

When you're writing a paper, don't think of yourself as a student working away at a school project. Think of yourself as a lawyer arguing an important case before a judge. By the trial's end, you want the judge (your instructor) to be absolutely convinced of your case, beyond any reasonable doubt. Like a lawyer, you'll present facts and evidence to support your case, in a clear, orderly, and persuasive fashion. And you'll want to argue your case as if somebody's life is on the line, filling each sentence with passion and meaning. It's impossible to simply sit down and write that kind of paper off the top of your head. Like a lawyer preparing for a big trial, working on your paper is going to take time and effort. That's why you need to think of writing as a process rather than a finished product — a process that starts the minute you get the assignment.

The Writing Process

You get an assignment from your teacher or professor for a major paper or essay. What are you going to do now? What is the general approach you take to the assignment?

Many students don't have a strategy for how to research and write a paper; when they get the assignment, they scramble like mad to knock out the paper without taking the time to consider what is the most effective and efficient way to go about the whole process. Are you like one of these students?

The First-Shot Writer

When the "First Shot" writer sits at her computer to type up her essay, she's already spent the last few days conducting research and taking notes so she has a definite idea about what she wants to write. She is confident that her ideas are quite sophisticated and will certainly impress the teacher. Typing up the essay takes about three hours. Certain the essay is excellent, she prints it out and staples it together without reading it again. When she gets it back, she finds she got a C. The teacher had questions about almost every paragraph and seemed to have completely missed her brilliant ideas.

The Over-Researched Writer

The "Over-Researcher" spends about a month meticulously researching his essay topic. He takes out scores of books and articles from the library and takes pages of notes on all of them. When he writes his essay, he makes certain to mention and quote from each and every source. However, rather than being impressed by all the research he's done, the teacher observes that there is not a single original idea in the essay. When the teacher meets with the student, she asks him, "What do *you* think about this topic?" and the Over-Researcher realizes he has no idea.

The Last-Minute Brainstorm Writer

The night before an essay is due, the "Brainstormer" sits at her computer. Off the top of her head, she begins writing. As she works, she thinks of more and more things to say about the topic, and she continues to write them down. After writing several paragraphs, she thinks of something new that relates to her first point. She then writes, "By the way, in reference to my earlier point, I also believe..." and expands upon that point. She then starts writing about something else that occurs to her. She spell-checks the document, prints it out, and turns it in. When she gets it back, the teacher has circled the last sentence of the essay and written: "This is the most powerful and original idea in your essay. You should have started with this point and spent the entire essay addressing this idea. I would have given you an A."

These students, while approaching the assignment in different ways, have all made similar mistakes — mistakes that too many students tend to make. In each case, they have not approached the paper using a carefully thought-out, organized, step-by-step process. As a result, they've left out important information that would have made the final essay much better. Working on a paper or essay is about much more than putting words on paper — you've got to think, research, organize, strategize, and clarify. That's a lot of work, and without a plan of action, you're bound to run into trouble.

This book outlines a step-by-step approach to writing essays that ensures your ideas are communicated in a clear, organized, and powerful manner. Each section highlights a different step in the process of writing an effective and well-organized paper. We'll begin by discussing how to come up with interesting and engaging topics and how you can learn more about those subjects. Then we'll discuss how to design the thesis statement — the central argument that will serve as the main point for your paper. As we'll see, the work you do in these early steps is crucial to how the finished essay will turn out. Next we'll examine various means of conducting and organizing research, from where to find source materials to tips on keeping track of the information you're gathering so you can bring it into the paper. From there, we'll concentrate on the structure of an effective paper, and see how it works not only to make your ideas clear to the reader but also to make your argument more powerful.

This book also includes an important section on research paper format, detailing the specifics of how to cite the source materials you are bringing in to support your argument. Using the correct format is crucial; it makes your paper clean and easy to read, and, especially important, it protects you from committing plagiarism. Finally, this book presents valuable tips that will help make your paper a solid piece of good writing.

By taking you step by step through the process of writing a paper, from settling on a topic to proofreading the final draft, this book will ensure that your work proceeds efficiently and productively. In fact, if you have a writing assignment right now, you can do it as you read this book. Each chapter focuses on a particular step in the writing process. Read each chapter and do the work required for that step. By the end of the book, you'll have a finished paper.

As a high school or college student, you'll probably have to write many essays as well as term papers and research papers. Generally, an essay is considered a shorter paper that focuses on a specific topic and/or expresses a personal viewpoint or argument, while a term paper or research paper is a longer work that draws on material from outside sources. The guidelines, strategies, and tips described in this book can help you write papers of all kinds, whether you are a high school or college student. Although a college research paper will be written on a more advanced level, the elements of an effective paper and the procedure for writing one do not differ between the high school and college levels. Many teachers insist that the student follow the method taught to them in class. While the writing methods that various instructors teach might differ slightly from the one this book describes, the guidelines and tips included here can still be enormously helpful in writing a paper.

Whatever you do, do not think about your writing assignment as a tedious exercise with limited relevance. Like the essay itself, the experience of writing depends on what you put into it. It will be a burden if you let it be. However, if you choose topics that interest you and if you understand that the skills involved in writing this essay can and will prove useful in many situations, you'll have a much more enriching experience. And your attitude will certainly show in the finished product.

Choosing a Topic and Brainstorming Ideas

Wanted: An Essay Topic

Choosing a topic can be the most difficult and challenging part of writing a paper. In many ways, it's also the most important step in the writing process because the topic you choose has a major effect on how the final product will turn out. It's pretty safe to say that an original and exciting topic will more likely result in an original and exciting essay. You should therefore be careful not to choose a topic haphazardly. Take the time to put some thought into the decision before you begin other work on the paper.

In selecting a topic, it's important to take into account the nature of the assignment and the requirements you receive from your teacher. Sometimes a teacher will assign a very specific topic and provide you with detailed requirements as to what the essay should address. However, even with the most rigidly defined assignment, you are going to have room to make your own decisions. In this case, the challenge is to view the subject from your own perspective and to somehow make it your own. Even if your instructor

Determine the essay requirements and your teacher's expectations.

has given you lots of information about the topic, you still need to spend time thinking about the assignment and how you plan to approach it in your own manner.

At other times, a teacher will suggest several topics or provide you with a very loosely defined assignment that gives you a great deal of freedom. Don't make the mistake of thinking that being allowed to choose your own topic makes the essay easier to write. Having free reign with an essay is exciting, but also overwhelming. There are so many possibilities for topics, how are you supposed to find one that's right for you — and the most impressive for the reader?

Variables to Consider

In choosing a topic, there are certain key factors that it's crucial for you to take into account. Thinking about these variables now can save you from hitting some major stumbling blocks further down the line in the writing process. They also ensure — right from the start of the writing process — that you are well on the way to a well-organized, lucid, and interesting essay.

What Interests You Most?
You are probably going to be spending a great deal of time and effort working on an essay. If the topic itself doesn't

ignite your interest, those hours are going to seem even longer and the writing process even more tedious. However, if you choose a subject that's important to you, or a subject you truly want to know more about, then the process of researching and writing the essay will be much more engaging — and feel much less like a chore.

When you receive the assignment, you might immediately hit on a topic that excites you. If that happens, go with it. If your gut reaction is that this is a topic you want to work on, you're probably right and should trust your instincts. However, if nothing immediately grabs you, don't be dismayed. It often takes time to settle on a subject about which you can feel passionate. If nothing comes to mind immediately, take some time to think more about what you've been studying so far. Think about the various themes and topics that have been addressed in class, as well as the reading assignments you've completed. Was there a particular subject that you enjoyed learning about? Was there anything you only touched on in class but that you wanted to know more about? Do you have a particular opinion or point of view about a topic you'd like to express? Did you have an intense emotional reaction to anything you read or discussed in class? Think about your gut reaction to material you've encountered in the course so far. If there was a particular work or lecture to which you had some kind of reaction — whether it be interest or even a negative reaction like confusion or anger — that's probably a good starting place for finding a more specific idea or topic to investigate. Any sort of emotional reaction to something you've been studying means that, on some level, it engaged you and peaked your interest. It's much better to start working on a paper about something that affected you that way than material or a subject about which you feel ambivalent.

Who Is Your Audience?

In addition to considering your own interests, you should also consider the expectations of your reader. All good writers try to direct their work specifically to their intended audience. An author of a children's picture book is going to write in a completely different manner from someone writing an accounting textbook; if the writer knows what he or she is doing, then the content and the writing style will suit the typical reader — either a child or an adult student — for those books. In the case of writing an essay, your primary reader is usually going to be the teacher or professor who assigned it to you and will grade it. Before you begin work, you need to make certain you understand the assignment and are aware of the teacher's expectations. Make certain you know the exact requirements for the essay given to you by the teacher. How much research, if any, should you be conducting? Do you need to refer to other sources? If so, how many? How long should the essay be? What format should you use for citing sources? Is there anything specific you should include or address?

You might consider setting up an appointment with your teacher, or going to talk during office hours, to try to gauge the teacher's expectations about the essay. If you engage your professor in a conversation about possible

Choose a topic that your teacher will find unique. Many teachers become bored reading about the same topics over and over again; most will therefore respect and welcome a paper written on something a bit more unusual.

topics, perhaps by running some of your ideas for the essay by him or her, you may be able to gain a sense of what your teacher particularly expects or looks for in grading the essays. Some teachers are most impressed by ambitious topics and ideas; others look for clarity and organization. Some want to see that you've conducted extensive research and can quote from many sources; others are more impressed by your individual ideas. See if you can gain a sense of what your teacher — the audience for this particular written work — is looking for.

If you are writing about a topic such as an historical event or literary work that has been discussed by others for centuries, it may seem difficult to be original. Be assured, though, that the *way* you write about the topic can in fact add a new twist to it that makes it seem original. Think about the many people who have written about love; that same topic has been addressed in an infinite number of interesting ways, depending on the style and perspective of the person who is writing about it.

Does the Topic Fit the Page Requirements?

For most essay assignments, the teacher will give some kind of page requirement, indicating the maximum and/or

Identify a broad subject area for your paper.

minimum number of pages you must turn in. You may not realize it, but this number should be a factor in choosing a topic. Good essays are ones that fully explore a particular topic in detail, without digressing into areas that are only marginally related. In order to write that kind of focused, comprehensive essay, you need to choose a topic that can be addressed fully within the page requirements set by the teacher.

If you choose a topic that is too broad for the paper's length requirements, you will then wind up writing about it in simplistic, superficial terms. You won't have the space to get into much detail, so the entire essay will remain on a broad and obvious level. For example, it would be difficult to write an essay on "The Poems of Emily Dickinson" in only six pages; you'd have to discuss each poem in about one or two lines in order to get to them all. Additionally, you might be biting off more than you can chew in terms of research. It would take you a long time just to read all of Dickinson's poems, much less write about them. You could, though, narrow that topic down to something more specific, such as a common theme or image in a few of Dickinson's poems. In so doing, you ensure you can write an essay that explores that topic in detail.

Students often initially choose topics that are too broad because they are concerned about meeting the page requirements. At first, writing six or seven pages sounds like a lot to have to "fill up," so you might choose a huge

It's okay to start out with a general, broad area of interest; as you read and think about the subject, you'll be able to narrow down your topic to something more specific.

topic to guarantee you have enough to write. However, once you begin thinking about and researching your topic at length, you'll find you have plenty of material. In fact, you may then find you need to decide what material to leave out. Don't worry about "filling up" pages; once you begin researching and/or generating ideas about your topic, you'll have plenty of material for an essay.

Choosing a topic that is too limited for the page requirements is also a problem. If your topic is too narrow, you may find yourself bending over backwards to meet the page requirements. Your paper then will be too wordy and repetitive. For example, it would be difficult to find enough original thoughts to express on a single Emily Dickinson poem in a twenty-five-page paper; you would probably run out of ideas after the first few pages and wind up repeating the same points over and over. Your topic should be broad enough so that you can fill the essay with strong ideas that keep the reader engaged. Most term papers will require broader topics than essays, as you are usually expected to conduct more extensive research over the course of a longer period of time.

Fine-Tuning the Topic

Choosing a topic appropriate for certain page requirements takes experience. In time, you'll gain an overall sense of what is an appropriate topic for a particular length of essay. Even so, most writers, even experienced ones, don't pull innovative and highly specified topics out of thin air.

Here is a list of general topics that would make a good starting point for an essay:

- A particular work of literature, article, or text, or a body of works you read in class
- An author, person, or a particular group of individuals you studied in your course
- An historical period or event, or a contemporary news event
- A literary period or genre
- A scientific field or subfield, in either the general sciences or social sciences
- A particular issue or subject of debate, either historical or contemporary

All of the above are broad subjects that would take lengthy papers in order to be fully examined. However, they all make fine starting points for essays; you can choose one and begin to think and read more about it. As you do, you'll gradually be able to narrow it down to a topic appropriate for the length of your essay. Remember to let yourself be flexible. Just because you've settled on a topic does not mean it has to remain that way forever. As you begin thinking about the topic and conducting research, feel free to redefine your topic, especially if you are tailoring it more to the page requirements for the essay.

Narrow and fine-tune subject to a focused topic appropriate for your essay's requirements.

Take the Plunge and Immerse Yourself

After you've chosen a general topic, you need to immerse yourself in the subject matter by reading and thinking about it at greater length. By doing this, you gain some basic knowledge about your subject and begin to narrow the general topic down to a more specific one. Most importantly, you begin to generate your own ideas about the topic, which are instrumental to a good essay.

Start by reading anything you can find that relates to your chosen subject. The reference section of a library is an ideal place to begin reading, as many general sources and resources are kept there. Generally, encyclopedias and almanacs are not considered appropriate sources for a research essay. You can, though, consult them at this early stage just to get some basic information about your overall topic. Make certain, though, that you pick a thorough, academic encyclopedia such as *Encyclopedia Britannica*, *Encyclopedia Americana*, or *Collier's Encyclopedia*.

You can also find many specialized dictionaries and encyclopedias that address specific fields, including ones for Arts and Entertainment, Science and Technology, Economics, Education, History, Literature, Mathematics, Psychology, Religion, and Social Sciences. If you're having trouble finding a source, you can always ask the reference librarian for suggestions.

Allow the topic to percolate a bit and start coming up with your own thoughts and ideas about it.

In addition to the reference section, you may want to search the stacks of the library for general books on your topic. You can use the library's index (either the card catalog or a computerized index; more information on finding sources in the library will follow) and search according to the subject. Pick any book listed under that subject and copy down the call number. All of the books related to that subject should be located in the same section of the library, so you can go to that section and browse. Pick a few books that seem interesting and read sections of them. You don't necessarily need to read the entire book. For example, reading the introduction to a book on your topic may provide you with a great deal of information. You can also check out bookstores; find the section of the store that has books related to your topic and browse the shelves. Anything related to your topic that catches your eye, flip through and skim. You might consider buying some of these books; most bookstores today, though, also let you read books in the store at length.

If you are writing an essay that centers on a specific text from class (such as a specific work of literature, a scientific theory or study, or a particular book or article), it is crucial that you reread that text several times. As you read, jot down any ideas that pop into your head about the text that might make a powerful contribution to an essay. Reading the original text a few times may provide you with enough information to begin to research and write an essay. However, if you find you are having difficulty, you may want to do some background reading about that text to help you brainstorm ideas of your own.

As you read about your topic, you'll find you start coming up with thoughts and ideas about it. Don't expect this to happen right away. The mind needs to let information sit for a while before it starts generating ideas. As you read about and immerse yourself in a subject, the information you ingest will percolate in your mind. You'll soon begin making connections with things you've learned, forming your own opinions and views, and gaining insight into the material. As you continue reading, your ideas and interests will become more focused and defined, and you will then be able to narrow down your topic.

Although you don't have to concern yourself just yet with taking detailed notes on sources, be sure you make a note of any ideas that pop into your head. That way, you'll be certain you remember them and include them in the essay.

EXERCISE:
BRAINSTORMING IDEAS AND TOPICS

At some point early in the writing stage, while you are initially immersing yourself in your subject or even just trying to fine-tune a topic, you can try this simple exercise to help brainstorm ideas. Sit at a desk or table with some blank sheets of paper, a pen, and a timer. Set the timer for five minutes. When the timer begins, start to write whatever ideas pop into your head related to your topic. The key is to keep writing without stopping for the entire five minutes. If you can't think of something to write, you can simply write down, "I don't know what to write" or rewrite something you have already put down on the paper. Don't worry about grammar or style or neatness. This is an exercise just for you; no one else will ever see it. When the timer stops, read over what you wrote, and underline anything that sounds interesting—a sentence or even just a word or phrase.

This exercise should help you get on paper some of the ideas that have been percolating in your mind but haven't yet come out in neat, fully formed sentences. You can repeat this exercise as many times as you like to generate more ideas. You might, for example, try taking a word or phrase from the first five-minute exercise and using it as the starting place for another five minutes. You'll be amazed at some of the interesting things that come up through this exercise.

Designing a Thesis Statement

Show a Little Backbone

The key to any good essay is the thesis statement. The thesis is the paper's central idea; it functions as the essay's backbone, holding together the various parts as a cohesive whole.

The thesis statement is not the same thing as your topic, although they are closely related. Your topic is a general subject that you've read and thought about to generate specific ideas. Based on that process, you should now be able to formulate a particular point of view about some aspect of the topic. This viewpoint, condensed into a single statement that sums up the central idea of the essay, is your thesis statement. Without the thesis statement, the essay is merely a random list of ideas, without any clear, definable point.

A thesis statement can simply be a sentence that states the central topic of the paper. Starting with this kind of basic thesis statement results in a straightforward essay that summarizes aspects of the subject matter. A more effective thesis statement reflects a specific viewpoint or opinion

> Every essay should have a thesis statement and all
> ideas expressed in the paper should relate to it.

about the subject matter; the essay, in turn, represents the detailed argument that supports this viewpoint. Most teachers are receptive to this kind of essay; they usually don't want to read a summary of factual information about a subject, but are interested in your own perspective. The more original the thesis statement, the more original — and impressive — your essay will be.

Components of an Effective Thesis Statement

In order to make your thesis statement effective, as in the sidebar examples, you should follow these guidelines:

Be specific.   An effective thesis statement is not too broad or general; instead, it should say something very specific about your topic. By being very specific, a thesis statement ensures that the essay remains focused and does not veer off into unrelated territory that distracts the reader.

Use your own ideas.   Most professors will be more impressed when you express your own thoughts and ideas rather then regurgitating someone else's. A more effective thesis statement will therefore be original and reflect your own outlook on the subject. Make certain the thesis is phrased entirely in your own words.

Sample topics and the effective thesis statements that might emerge from them:

Topics:
- American Literature of the 1920s
- Modern Psychological Theories and Treatments
- The Cold War

Thesis Statements:
- Most American literature of the 1920s depicts a growing anxiety regarding the dehumanizing effects of industrialization.
- Although dreams play a central role in both Freudian and Jungian theory, there are crucial differences in the ways in which dreams are interpreted.
- The foreign policy of the United States during the Cold War indirectly served to escalate domestic problems on American soil.

State something you believe. The body of the essay must make a convincing argument supporting the thesis statement. However, it is extremely difficult to present a solid argument supporting an idea that you don't believe is true. Moreover, if the thesis statement reflects a personal belief, the entire essay will bear the strength of your convictions. Don't work against the grain and choose a thesis statement that you don't support.

Be sure you can build an argument. Your goal in writing the essay is to convince your reader that your thesis statement is an accurate one; you want to prove your viewpoint beyond a shadow of a doubt. Therefore, make certain you pick a thesis you know you can prove with a solid supporting argument. When you begin conducting research, you may find you now don't necessarily agree with or can't prove your original thesis. If this is the case, change the thesis statement.

Phrase your thesis in a single, direct sentence. As we've said, most essays for academic purposes are limited in length; you probably won't have to write an entire book-length dissertation at this stage. You therefore don't need a long, detailed thesis statement. Make certain you can phrase your thesis statement in one sentence. If you can't do it in one sentence, it either indicates you are unfocused and confused about your idea, or that you've chosen a thesis too ambitious to be proven in a single essay.

Fine-Tuning the Thesis Statement

Like your topic, you may need to take some time to fine-tune your thesis statement. Until you've actually begun writing, it is fine to have only a general sense of your thesis. As you conduct research and gain more knowledge of your topic, you'll continue to hone your thesis statement. Try rewriting and revising the thesis statement in several different ways. Try using a variety of words, or ordering the words in the sentence in different patterns. The thesis is probably the single most important sentence in the essay; it's worth taking the time to get it exactly the way you want it.

Once you have an idea of what your thesis statement will be, it's a good idea to discuss it with your teacher. This will make certain you are on the right track. Your teacher may also have suggestions, based on the thesis statement, as to how to conduct research and organize the essay.

Conducting Research

Types of Essays/Types of Sources

There are essentially two kinds of essays: ones that require you to do research from outside sources, and ones that do not. Essays that do not require research focus solely on your own thoughts and ideas about a particular topic; those that include research use information from outside sources to explain and/or support your thesis. Your teacher probably will tell you whether or not you are expected to do research and include other sources in your essay. If the teacher doesn't tell you, then ask. If you are working on an essay that does not require you to work with sources, you can skip ahead to the chapter on essay structure.

For other types of essays, there are two kinds of sources you might need to refer to and write about in the essay: *primary* and *secondary sources*. Primary sources are any texts that are the focus of an essay, such as specific works of literature, historical documents, or essays and articles on certain theories and philosophies. For example, if you are writing about some of Shakespeare's plays, then *Romeo and Juliet* and *Hamlet* would serve as primary sources for the essay. Laboratory studies and data generated in scientific studies can also be considered primary sources. If your essay centers on a primary source, you must make certain you read it in detail and take notes on it. You can still use many of the techniques outlined in this and the next section for reading and taking notes on sources.

Many papers also incorporate information from secondary sources. These are often called research papers or term papers, because conducting research, reading a variety of sources, and including that information in the paper is a major requirement. Secondary sources include books and articles by critics, historians, scholars, and other writers who comment on and address primary sources as well as other topics and subjects. The techniques outlined in this chapter will show you how to track down secondary sources that address your topic and how to take notes on them.

Identifying Possible Sources

There are obviously going to be many sources that address your topic and/or thesis. However, before you can read them, you need to identify them and then go find them. It would waste a lot of time and be stressful just to wander around a library or bookstore hoping you'll find something useful. It makes much more sense to create a list of possible sources you think you'd like to consult and then go look specifically for those works. But how are you supposed to know what those sources are? Fortunately, there are several resources you can turn to for help in identifying possible sources relevant to your topic and/or thesis.

The Library Subject Catalog

All libraries list their holdings in a catalog. Some have index cards kept in file drawers called the card catalog, but more and more libraries list their holdings on computer terminals in an on-line catalog (more on this follows). The entries in the catalog are usually organized three ways: by author, title, and subject. If you have a specific source in mind, you can consult the author or title entry to find out if the library has the source and where it is located. If you are merely looking for general sources, though, you can search according to the subject.

Most libraries organize their subject catalogs according to the standard list of subjects set by the Library of Congress, although some libraries have their own classifications. The library should have a subject list available for you to consult. Sometimes a subject will be divided into subcategories. Try to find whatever subject or subcategory most closely relates to your topic.

You can then go to the catalog and scan the list of titles within a particular subject or subcategory and look for any that seem relevant or interesting. However, it may be difficult to judge a source based just on the title. A more effective method is to find one title and look up the call number. You can then go to that section of the library and browse the shelves. Usually all the books on a particular subject will be grouped together, so you should be able to find several sources in that section.

Published Bibliographies and Indexes

There are many published bibliographies and indexes that list books and other sources, such as academic journals and periodical articles, on a particular subject. For example, there is a separate published bibliography for almost every one of Shakespeare's plays that lists secondary sources for that play only. For many subjects, there will be some kind of bibliography that addresses that specific topic.

Bibliographies compile citations for various books and sources. A citation is a bibliographic listing for a particular source that provides key information — author, title and publication information — that will help you locate the source. Annotated bibliographies are especially helpful, as they also list a brief description for each source included.

Published bibliographies are usually located within the reference section of the library. To find a bibliography on your topic, you can either ask the reference librarian for suggestions or use the catalog. Under many of the subjects in the subject catalog, there will be a subcategory that lists bibliographies for that subject.

In order to find periodical sources, you can use specialized *indexes*, which primarily list citations for journal and magazine articles and essays within larger works. The indexes will list the articles, usually by subject, while *abstracts* will also include brief descriptions of the articles.

SAMPLE ANNOTATED CITATION

Rabkin, Norman. *Shakespeare and the Common Under-standing*. New York: Free Press, 1967. 267 pp.

The true constant of Shakespearean tragedy is the dialectical dramaturgy, and *King Lear* provides one of the most powerful examples. The universe envisioned by the stage world is subject to contradictory interpretations.

As with bibliographies, there are general indexes as well as specialized indexes that cover specific topics. The index will list a citation for an article, displaying the key information on the source, such as the author, title of the periodical in which it can be found, the periodical's year, volume, and issue number, and the pages where the article can be found. Most magazine and journal titles are abbreviated, and a key to the abbreviations will be at the front of the index.

Major Indexes and Bibliographic Sources. Here is a listing of some of the major indexes and bibliographies that might be helpful in your search for sources. Most can be found in the reference room of any library; many can also be found on the Internet. These are only very general indexes. There are also many bibliographies that are tailored to specific subjects, topics, and fields that you can consult and that might match with your particular topic.

General

- *Books in Print* — A listing of all books still in print and currently published in the U.S., separated by author, subject, title, publisher, and forthcoming titles. Published annually.
- *Essay and General Literature Index* — An index to essays that appear in books of collected essays and anthologies in the fields of humanities and social sciences. Organized by author and subject. Updated semiannually.
- *Reader's Guide to Periodical Literature* — This is the primary index to articles in popular magazines. Approximately two hundred different magazines (general, news, entertainment, popular interest, etc.) are indexed. Organized by subject and author. Updated biweekly.

Arts, Humanities, and Literature

- *Annual Bibliography of English Language and Literature* — Indexes secondary sources for all literature in English, categorized by century. New editions are published every year.
- *Humanities Index* — An index of articles appearing in approximately 350 academic journals and some popular periodicals in the humanities. Categorizes articles by theme, genre, author, and topic, and includes a listing of book and theater reviews. Updated quarterly.
- *MLA International Bibliography of Books and Articles on the Modern Languages and Literatures* — An extremely comprehensive listing of secondary

sources for literature from all periods. It indexes books, articles in journals, and essays in anthologies and compilations.

Biography
- *Biography & Genealogy Master Index* — Does not include biographical information on personalities, but indexes biographical sources and studies.
- *Biography Index* — Lists books and over two thousand periodicals on various biographical sources, with a subject index. Updated quarterly.
- *Who's Who* — Lists key information (date of birth, education, spouse, children, occupations, title, etc.) regarding various prominent personalities. There are several different versions of *Who's Who*, including American and International editions.

History
- *Historical Abstracts* — An index to over two thousand historical journals, now covering 1450 to the present.
- *International Bibliography of Historical Sciences* — An index to books and articles on all historical periods.

News and Current Events
- *Facts on File* — Includes summaries of major news events — national and international — indexed by subject. Updated weekly.
- *Newspaper Indexes* — Many major newspapers, such as the *New York Times* and the *Wall Street Journal*,

have their own indexes that will often be organized by subject heading. There is also a National Newspaper Index that incorporates several major newspapers in one index.

There are also indexes to book and theater reviews in certain newspapers, such as the *New York Times* and the *London Times*.

Sciences
- *General Science Index* — An index of articles appearing in academic journals and periodicals from all fields in the general sciences. Updated quarterly.
- *Social Sciences Index* — An index of articles appearing in academic journals and some periodicals in the social sciences, organized by subject and author, and with a separate listing of book reviews. Updated quarterly.

Lists of Works Cited and Bibliographies in Sources

Most academic books, essays, and journals include their own bibliographies, list of works cited, or suggested further readings. These listings can provide you with suggestions for sources you might like to read as part of your research. Each time you read a new book or article, be certain to check the author's bibliography or notes to see if there is anything you might like to consult yourself. You can also check the assigned readings for your course, such as your textbook and other articles selected by your teacher, to see if there are lists of sources.

Computerized Information Resources

Several of the indexes listed here, such as the *MLA Bibliography* and the *Reader's Guide to Periodical Literature*, are available on computer. Many libraries have computer monitors set up that enable you to access these various databases to conduct on-line searches. You can instruct the computer to search for sources relating to a particular author, title, or subject, and the computer will put together and print out a listing for you. Libraries have different regulations for conducting on-line searches. Some might require that you meet with a librarian to learn about the system before you use it on your own. You might also have to sign up for time to work on the computer.

The Internet is a valuable tool for finding sources, provided you know how to use it and have access to it. If you have access to the Internet, either at home or at the school's computer center, you can surf the net to look for sources. Through the Internet, you can gain access to indexes and bibliographies, and also find entire articles from newspapers, magazines, and periodicals. Many schools and school libraries offer special classes or seminars in how to conduct on-line research and searches. Ask your teacher or librarian if such a program exists.

There are also many published guides and books that include simple directions for using the Internet for a variety of purposes, including conducting research. Here is a list of some basic guidebooks that are particularly accessible for beginners.

Internet for Dummies by John Levine, Carol Baroudi, and Margaret Levine Young (IDG Books)

The Internet for Everyone by Richard Wiggins (McGraw Hill)

The Complete Idiot's Guide to the Internet by Peter Kent (QUE Books)

Everybody's Guide to the Internet by Adam Griffin (MIT Press)

The Internet Guide for New Users by Daniel P. Dern (Prentice-Hall)

The Internet Navigator by Paul Gilster (Wiley)

Internet for School Work: The following books are particularly useful for students, as they contain specific sections on academic uses of the Internet:

Internet 101: A College Student's Guide by Alfred Glossbrenner (McGraw Hill)

The Internet for Teachers by Bard Williams (IDG Books)

Reference Books: The following books list sites on the Internet. They can be quite helpful in finding information on the Internet more quickly and efficiently.

The Internet Yellow Pages (NRP)

The World Wide Web Yellow Pages (NRP)

The Internet Directory by Eric Braun (Fawcett)

Computer Magazines: The following magazines include a wealth of information and special tips on using the Internet and other computer technology. You can find them in the library or bookstore.

Wired
Internet World

Keeping Track of Sources: Using Bibliography Cards

It's a good idea to first come up with a list of possible sources you might like to check out — consulting the reference sources listed above — and then look for them in various places such as the library, bookstore, or on the Internet. That way you can focus your searches more directly and cut down on the number of trips you'll make to get sources.

Whenever you find a reference to a source you think you might like to investigate, make a note of it. It is extremely important that you write down all relevant information about the source, including the author(s), title, publisher (for a book), volume and date (for a periodical or journal), and anthology name and editor (for an essay or article included in another work). This information helps you to find the source and is also necessary when you create your final bibliography.

You can keep your list of sources in a notebook or on a legal pad. However, a particularly efficient way to organize this information is to make bibliography cards. You simply

SAMPLE BIBLIOGRAPHY CARD

Call Number: PN2023.5

Stevens, Jay Q. *Shakespeare on the Contemporary American Stage*. New York: Publishers Press, 1995.

Location: General Stacks, Fifth Floor

Summary: Reviews and analyzes several contemporary U.S. productions of Shakespeare's plays,

— Specific productions include *The Tempest* and *Troilus and Cressida*.

— Compares American vs. British production styles.

fill out a separate 3x5 index card for each source that includes all of the relevant publication information. The cards provide you with greater flexibility; you can arrange them in any order you please, such as alphabetically or in order of importance. You can also group various cards to make your research more organized. For example, if you are going to a particular library or bookstore to look for sources, you only need to bring those cards with you. Finally, the cards provide you with extra room to take brief notes that will help you find the source, such as the call number or general location in the library.

As you will probably be reading a large number of sources, it is suggested that you also write a brief summary of each work that you read. These summaries will be especially helpful if you later need to return to a particular source in order to find a specific point. Either at the bottom or on the back of the bibliography card, write a one or two line summation of the article or book. What seems to be the purpose of the material? What is it seeking to prove? See if you can identify the source's thesis statement and write that down. Beneath it, you might also want to list the essential points that the source makes.

It's a good idea to get in the habit of listing the source on each card in the correct bibliographic format (see chapter on citing sources). By doing this, you ensure that you have all the required information on the card that you will need for your final bibliography. It can be a real pain to have to go back to the library at the last minute to get information on a particular source. You might need to wait until you have a source in your hands to include some of the specific information, such as the publisher or copyright information. You can fill that in directly on the card once you have the source. You can also include additional notes to help you as you conduct your search for materials, such as a book's call number (from the catalog) or the floor of the library where it is located.

Tracking Down Sources

Once you've found out about a source that you think will be helpful, you then need to track it down so you can read it, take notes on it, and possibly use it in your essay. When you've got a list or bibliography cards for several sources, you can start to search for them. There are several places where you can search for sources.

In the Library

The library — either a public library or your school library — is the main place to go for sources. You're more likely to find a wide range of academic sources you'll need for your essay at the library, and you won't have to pay anything to get them. You should learn how to use the library to your advantage. Think of the library as your office while you work on researching your essay. Take the time to learn your way around and feel comfortable there. Most libraries are rich in resources; you just need to find out what they are. You might consider taking a library tour or attending an orientation session; if there isn't one available, wander around on your own. You can always feel free to ask librarians for help or suggestions; that's what they're there for.

Seek out and use the best library that is available to you. A college or university library will probably have a more extensive and academic collection and better resources than a local public library. However, the main branch of the public library in most cities will have a large collection of sources and varied services. You may need to check several libraries to find all the sources you need; not every library is going to have every source you're looking for.

Card Catalogs.   To track down most sources in the library you need to learn how to use the library's central catalog. Many libraries still have their catalogs on cards. The information in the card catalog is usually indexed by author, title and subject. In most libraries, the author and title cards will be grouped together in the same area, and the subject cards will be separated in a different section of drawers. In some libraries, the author, title, and subject cards will all be grouped together alphabetically within the same catalog.

For each book in the library, there will be a separate author, title, and subject card in the catalog. This enables you to find a book even if you do not have all the information about it. For example, you may know the title of a certain work but do not remember the author. By using the title cards, you will still be able to find the book. Similarly, you may want to see what works a particular author has written. By examining the author cards, you will be able to see names of all the books by that author within the library.

The subject category is especially helpful when you begin your quest for sources. It enables you to look for information even if you do not have a particular book in mind. Most libraries organize their subject catalog according to the list of standard subjects set by the Library of Congress, although some libraries use their own subject classifications. The library should have a subject list available that you can consult. After identifying the subject in which your topic falls, you can then look it up in the subject catalog to find whatever relevant books the library has.

The cards in the catalog all detail basic information about the book, including author, title, subject, publication information, author's date of birth, and number of pages. Most importantly, the card will also indicate the book's location within the library. Most libraries are organized according to either the Dewey decimal system or the

In many libraries' computer catalogs, you do not even need to know the full title of a work in order to find it. You can begin a search by entering key words from the title. The screen will then display all of the titles that have those key words in it.

Library of Congress system. These systems use combinations of numbers and letters to indicate a book's subject and location in the library. In the card catalog, a combination of letters and numbers will appear in the top left-hand corner of the card. This is known as the call number, and it is based upon the system of organization the library uses. Each book within the library has a call number, and you use it to locate the book (see "Searching the Stacks" on the following page). Always be certain to copy down the call number.

On-Line Catalogs. Many libraries are now also putting their central catalogs onto a computer, which is known as the on-line catalog. In libraries that have an on-line catalog, there will usually be several computer terminals close to the card catalog to which the public has access. Most on-line systems are very easy to use and do not require much computer knowledge. There will probably be instructions by the terminals or a HELP function on the keyboard that will show you what to do. As with anything in the library, you can always ask a librarian for help. Once you become familiar with the on-line catalog, you'll find it is much easier and faster to use than the card catalog.

On-line catalogs are organized similarly to card catalogs. In most on-line systems, the first step will be to indicate whether you wish to conduct your search by author, title, or subject. Different computer systems use different commands and codes that you will have to use to indicate how you want to proceed. Again, the HELP function or some kind of written instructions should be available.

Once you have indicated how you want to conduct your search, a prompt on the screen will appear requesting you to enter the author, title, or subject for which you are searching.

One advantage of using the online system is that you do not usually need full information on the source in order to conduct a search. For example, if you enter an author's last name, the screen will display a list of full names for all authors with that last name, sometimes with their dates of birth. This information can help you pinpoint the right author. When you have selected a name from the list, the screen will then display a list of works by that author.

To conduct a subject search, you must enter a subject heading from the library's list of subject classifications or the computer system will not recognize the command. Consult the list of subjects in order to find the one most relevant to your topic. The system may allow you then to choose from subcategories within the subject to make your search easier.

Once you have selected the title you are interested in, a screen will appear that will display the same information as is included in the card catalog. The primary advantage of using the on-line catalog is that in addition to displaying general information about the book and the book's location, it will also indicate the status of the book. The screen might show if the book is in the library, on loan, or missing, and in some cases, when the book is due back.

Many on-line catalogs will enable you to print out hard copies of the information that appears on the screen. This can be extremely helpful both in tracking down sources and for when you later prepare your bibliography.

Searching the Stacks. The bulk of the library's resources consists of books which are housed in "stacks," meaning on the shelves. In some libraries, the public is denied access to the stacks. In these libraries, you should fill out a request slip with the call number and turn it in to the librarian. The book will then be retrieved for you.

In most libraries, the public has access to the stacks. In that case, you'll be free to search the library's shelves for whatever sources you need. First find the book's call number, from either the card catalog or the on-line catalog. Copy the call number from the card or computer screen (if you're using bibliography cards, you can copy the information directly onto the card). You can then either ask a librarian where it will be or try to track it down yourself. Most libraries are organized according to either the Dewey decimal system or the Library of Congress system (used in most colleges and universities). The Dewey decimal system groups books according to ten major headings, each one given its own number. The first few digits of a book's call

Librarians are the most vital resource in the library; they can provide you with a tremendous amount of help for just about any academic project you pursue. Ask them questions; that's what they're there for.

number, listed before the decimal point, will indicate this subject heading and will give you an idea of the general section of the library in which the book will be shelved. The digits following the decimal point more specifically indicate the exact location of the book.

Once you are in the general area, the books will be shelved in numerical order. There should be cards or signs that indicate the range of call numbers in each row of shelves. The numbers will be printed on the books' spines, and you can search down the row until you match the call number.

The Library of Congress system is organized in a similar manner but separates books into twenty major categories, each one given a letter or combination of letters. The first few letters in the call number will indicate the subject and the general area in which the book will be shelved, while the later digits will more specifically indicate the book's exact location.

If a book is not located where it should be, do not necessarily give up your search. Libraries are busy places and people are constantly shuffling around the shelves. Look for the book in the surrounding area, checking other shelves, books lying around or near the location, and nearby desks, tables, and book carts.

If you still cannot find the book and it is a vital source for your paper, go to the circulation desk and ask for help. The librarian may be able to check whether the book has been returned but has not yet been shelved, or tell you when it is due back. Some libraries will allow you to put a book "on hold," which means that when the book is returned, it will be held aside for you and you will be notified that the book is in. Some libraries, especially at colleges and universities, can have a book recalled if it has been out longer than the due date.

Other Book Locations in the Library. Not all books will be located in the general stacks. Many might be in the reference section of the library. Reference books must remain in the library and may not be checked out. The call number will usually be preceded by "REF" or "R" in order to indicate that the book is a reference book, shelved in the reference section of the library.

Oversized books are also often shelved separately. The catalog entry should indicate if a book is oversized. You can then ask a librarian where the oversized books are shelved.

In university libraries, professors often put books "on reserve," which means that they are kept in a separate section so that students in that course may borrow the book for a limited amount of time. In this case, the catalog entry should say On Reserve. You can go to the reserve desk and ask to see the book.

Other Sources, Resources, and Services in the Library. In addition to books, libraries house many other research materials, including newspapers, magazines, journals, videotapes, audiotapes, slides, and maps. These materials will usually be kept within their own sections of the library, which will often be indicated in the catalog entry. You can ask the librarian or check the library directory to see where these materials are located.

Due to the enormous space newspapers and magazines would consume and the problem of decay, libraries only keep them for a limited time period. Current newspapers and periodicals are usually kept in a separate area or room.

Magazines, periodicals, and scholarly journals are sometimes bound together into volumes and shelved in the stacks. (This is why bibliographies list a volume number in addition to the date of a periodical.) Bound volumes will usually be grouped in the same area in the library.

After a certain period of time, newspapers and most journals and magazines are transformed into a type of microform. Through a special process, the entire newspaper or magazine is miniaturized and put onto film. This process enables enormous amounts of material to be stored within a very small space. There are various types of microform, the most popular being microfilm, a long, thin strip of film that is rolled up, and microfiche, which is a single, transparent sheet.

The microforms are usually kept in a separate room. If a catalog entry says MICRO, or if you know you are looking for a periodical or journal that would be on microform, go directly to the microform room. There will usually be a librarian there to help you. In most libraries, you need a

Libraries offer many special resources and services worth knowing about, such as:

- Typewriter or Computer Centers
- Copy machines or Copy Services
- Audio/Visual Screening/Listening Facilities
- Language Labs
- Quiet Study Lounges and Cubicles
- Lockers
- Searches for Lost Books
- Holds Placed on Books Currently Checked Out
- Computers with Access to the World Wide Web
- Computerized Catalogs and Bibliographies

librarian to get the microform for you, although in some you can get them yourself from a file cabinet. Make certain you know the exact date of the periodical so that you can find the right microform.

As a result of the miniaturization process that is used, the print on microforms is too small to see with the naked eye. In order to read the material, you need to use a special monitor, which will probably be in the same room where the microforms are kept. There are usually a limited number of monitors and you will often have to wait. Find out if there is a sign-up sheet. The first few times you work on the monitors, you will probably need a librarian to show you how to use them.

Some monitors will enable you to make photocopies of different pages as they appear on the screen. You may want to use one of these machines, as it is easier to take notes from paper rather than reading from a screen. Having copies also enables you to spend more time with the source on your own.

Audiotapes and videotapes are often classified according to their own system. The library might have a separate catalog, brochure, or booklet listing titles, subjects, and artists, that you can consult.

Recalls/Interlibrary Loans. If a book or source you need is checked out, or not owned by the library, you don't need to despair. The library can still help you out. If a book is taken out by someone else, many libraries will enable you to recall the book. That means the person who has the book will get a note requesting it be returned; it will then be put on hold for you to pick up. If the library doesn't have the source you need, many will enable you to borrow a source from another library (usually at a minimal fee). Ask at the circulation desk or in the reference library how you can get an interlibrary loan.

Outside the Library

If you cannot find a particular source at your local library, you might consider purchasing the book. Contact several bookstores, particularly college bookstores, those that specialize in used books, or on-line bookstores like Amazon.com to see if they carry the book or can order it for you. You can also try calling the publisher and special ordering it. One volume of Books in Print lists publishers with addresses and phone numbers. You can also approach your instructor, who might own the very source for which you are so desperately searching. At the very least, the instructor should be able to make suggestions to help you find it.

How to End the Research Process

Once you have several sources, you can begin to read them and take notes (using techniques outlined in the next section). However, that will most likely only be the start of the research process. As you read the sources you have, you will probably be disappointed with some and come across others you'll want to consult. You also might realize you need new or additional information based on what you've already learned. Be prepared to make several trips in search of new materials as you conduct research.

At some point, though, you have to decide you've got enough sources and are ready to write the paper. It's easy to get so interested in research that you just keep reading new sources rather than write the paper. Keep the essay's deadline in mind, and determine a point when you will focus solely on organizing your notes and writing and revising the essay.

References Worth Owning

There are certain reference guides that every student should own — they are well worth the investment. These books will prove themselves indispensable as you study, from helping when you write essays and papers to enabling you to look up additional information as you read required texts and your classroom notes.

Collegiate Dictionary

This is the most important reference book for a student to own. As you go about your required reading for courses, you'll encounter many new vocabulary words that you'll need to know in order to follow what you read. Additionally, as you write essays, you should double-check the spelling and meaning of any words for which you are not 100 percent certain of the correct usage.

Thesaurus (Preferably in Dictionary Format)

The Thesaurus is a key tool for improving your writing. By looking up synonyms for words you use frequently, you can vary your word usage and make your writing much more interesting.

Specialized Dictionary

There are many specialized dictionaries on the market that list words, names, and terms within specific subjects, such as dictionaries of literary terms, scientific terms, mythology, etc. Depending on what area you study, you may wish to purchase one or several of these guides.

World Atlas

You'd be surprised how much information you can get from a good atlas. As you read or write, you can dip into the atlas for various facts, from identifying capitals to correct spellings of countries and cities. As you come across names of places in your reading, it doesn't hurt to gain a sense of where they are located.

Grammar Handbook

Turning in essays that are grammatically correct is extremely important; using proper grammar sends the message to your teacher that you are a serious student who takes pride in your work. Of course, there are so many different grammatical rules and exceptions, it is difficult to know them all by heart. If you own a good grammar handbook, you can dip into it and double-check any rules that give you trouble.

Style and/or Essay Format Manual

In addition to writing with proper grammar, it is also important that you be consistent in your writing style and format. You need to be consistent first and foremost in how you cite outside sources and list them in your bibliography. Depending on which format your teacher instructs you to follow, make certain you purchase a format guide, such as the MLA or APA handbook. In addition to citations, you also need to be consistent throughout your writing in your punctuation and language usage, such as what you capitalize or hyphenate. A style book, such as the *New York Times Manual of Style and Usage*, will list these pieces of information.

Almanac

Owning an almanac may seem silly, but you'll be surprised how much you can get out of it. You never know when you'll need some tidbit of information for a paper you're writing. The almanac can provide miscellaneous facts and figures, from past academy award winners to a list of the U.S. presidents and their birthplaces.

Reading Sources and Taking Notes

Is It Worth the Effort?

When you've tracked down a particular source, take a few moments to glance through it to determine whether it is relevant to your topic and can contribute significantly to your essay. Read the preface or introduction of a book, or the first few paragraphs of an article and try to identify the main argument or viewpoint of the piece. Try to determine whether it is well-written and accurate, the arguments are solidly supported, and the author seems qualified and knowledgeable.

If you decide a source might contribute to your essay, you need to read it very carefully and take notes on what you read. Many of these notes will eventually become vital parts of the essay, so it is extremely important that you take them accurately. Being organized with your note taking now will make the process of writing the essay easier later on.

Don't overlook terms or points that confuse you or that you do not remember well — especially those that seem particularly important to the subject. Keep a list of troublesome topics and lingering questions.

What Exactly Is Noteworthy?

When you are reading a particular source, you may not be certain what to take notes on. Sources can be quite long; how do you know what is relevant and worth noting and what isn't?

The most important thing to look for is anything that supports your thesis statement. Essentially, you are looking for hard evidence that you can use in the essay to argue in favor of your thesis. However, you can also take notes on anything that relates to your general topic, as these notes will help you develop a broad background knowledge of the field and might be used in the essay. Also, take notes on anything that intrigues you or sounds interesting. You won't necessarily use all of these notes in the essay. However, it is much easier to take notes first and throw them out later than have to reread sources to find information you came across earlier.

In the initial stages of conducting research, you may not have entirely formulated your thesis or conceived of the overall points your essay will make. You therefore may be uncertain as to what notes to take. It can be helpful to read a sampling of the sources you've tracked down before beginning to take notes. This will enable you to develop a background knowledge in the subject, which in turn will

> Decide which sources are most relevant or helpful to your topic.

help you fine-tune your thesis. When you have a better idea of the shape of your essay, you can then go back to various sources, to reread them more carefully and take notes.

By the way, if your essay uses primary sources, you need to read these carefully and take notes on them as well. Notes and quotations from primary sources are particularly strong pieces of evidence, especially if writing about a primary source is the focus of your essay.

What Exactly Do You Write Down?

Direct Quotations and Paraphrases

There are two types of notes derived from sources: *quotations* and *paraphrases*. A quotation restates a passage or a part of a passage from a source in the original writer's *exact words*. A paraphrase, on the other hand, restates the ideas in a passage, rephrased in *your own* words.

When you are reading a source and come across a sentence or passage you think is relevant, decide whether or not you want to quote it or paraphrase it. You should generally paraphrase more often than you quote. It is too tedious and time-consuming to copy down long passages word for word. However, if a sentence or passage is written in a particularly interesting or powerful manner that you think will stand well on its own in the essay, then you should copy it down as a quotation.

If you decide to quote a source, you need to copy the line or lines exactly as they appear in the original source. Be sure you put the lines in quotation marks. To be certain you remember that the note is a quotation, you may even want to write down "quotation from original" in parentheses next to the line. If you want to leave out part of a quotation because it is not relevant, you can use an ellipsis to indicate a word or phrase has been deleted. An ellipsis consists of either three spaced periods if the omitted word or passage is within a sentence, or four spaced periods if the word or passage comes at the end of a sentence.

Sometimes, when you take a quotation out of context, it won't make sense on its own and will need some clarification. If you decide to add a word or phrase to the quotation, you must put it in brackets to indicate that the word is not originally a part of the quotation.

If you decide to paraphrase the source, you must rephrase it *completely in your own words*. Make certain that your paraphrase is an accurate restatement of the main point of the passage.

Occasionally, you might want to quote a few words or a particular phrase within a paraphrase. For example, if the author has coined a particular term or described something in a unique way, be sure you quote those words exactly. However, you don't necessarily need to quote the entire paragraph. You can paraphrase the gist of the passage and include only a few words and phrases in quotation marks.

EXAMPLES OF QUOTATIONS AND PARAPHRASES

Original Source:
"More often than not, American productions of Shakespeare's plays in the 1990s have relocated the setting and changed the time period from the original, ranging from a version of *Richard III* set in Italy under Mussolini, to a futuristic version of *The Tempest* set on a faraway planet. At best, these relocations serve to enhance and expand the plays' inherent themes; at worst, they are flashy gimmicks that serve to obscure and confuse."

Quotation in Notes:
"More often than not, American productions of Shakespeare's plays in the 1990s have relocated the setting and changed the time period from the original....At best, these relocations serve to enhance and expand the plays' inherent themes; at worst, they are flashy gimmicks that serve to obscure and confuse." (quotation from original)

Paraphrase in Notes:
Productions of Shakespeare in the 1990s change the scene or time period. Sometimes the change is positive and adds something, but at others it only makes things confusing.

Partial Paraphrase/Partial Quotation of Source:
Productions of Shakespeare in the 1990s change the scene or time period. Sometimes the change can "enhance and expand" the original themes; at others, the changes are "gimmicks" that "obscure and confuse" the theme.

Indirect Quotations and Paraphrases

Occasionally, you may have to quote or paraphrase a part of a source in which that author has quoted or paraphrased someone else. This is known as an *indirect quotation*. If you use these notes later on when you write the paper, you'll need to clearly indicate both the source in which you found the quote, and the original speaker and or source that was quoted. You should therefore take very careful notes on these passages. If you are quoting, copy down the section exactly as it appears, putting the quotations within the passage in single quotation marks to indicate there is a quotation within the quotation. For both quotations and paraphrases, be certain to copy down the author's name and the title of the source that your source indirectly mentions. You may have to look carefully for this information, either in the source's bibliography, in previous footnotes, or previous chapters of a book.

Being a Careful Note Taker

Whenever you take down notes from a source, you also need to make certain you mark which source the material comes from and the exact page number(s). It is important that you take these notes carefully, as you must include this information in the essay whenever you use another source (you'll learn how to do that later in this book). If you don't acknowledge the original source in the essay, you are committing *plagiarism*. In writing your paper, taking care to avoid committing plagiarism should be your primary concern.

Read through sources and take notes — preferably on note cards — of anything in support of your thesis, relevant to your topic, or that interests you in general.

Most people think of plagiarism as when a student copies from or steals another student's paper. Such blatant cases of plagiarism are the most serious and can result in expulsion from school or even legal action. What many people do not realize, however, is that there are many less blatant cases of plagiarism that may be unintentional on the part of the writer. Writing a research paper differs significantly from other writing assignments in that you not only are allowed to use other writers' material, but are encouraged to do so. But you must always give credit where credit is due. Anytime in an essay you include an idea or a phrase from another source but do not credit the original source, you are committing plagiarism. Be certain to read the sections of this book on paper format and crediting sources.

There are two points in the paper-writing process where you must be especially careful so as to avoid accidentally committing plagiarism. One is when you document sources in the body of your paper. The other is when you are originally taking your notes, which eventually become the building blocks of your essay. This is why it is crucial that you take very precise notes and keep them organized. Make certain in your notes that you always identify the source and page number.

Plagiarism occurs when a writer uses someone else's ideas or words but does not give the original writer credit and instead passes off the material as his or her own. Committing plagiarism is regarded as an extremely serious act that, if caught, can have severe consequences.

Be especially careful when you paraphrase or quote from an outside source in your notes. If you paraphrase something, it must be completely rephrased in your own words and then attributed to the source. If a writer coins a particular phrase or describes something in an unusual way and you want to use it, you must put it in quotation marks. This even applies to single words, when the author uses them to describe something in an unusual or innovative way, as in the following example:

Source:
Milton's epic begins with a rush.
[From page 1445 of *The Norton Anthology of English Literature*, Vol. 1. 5th Edition.]

Plagiarized in Notes:
Paradise Lost begins with a rush.

The above note would be considered plagiarism because the word "rush," an unusual way to describe the beginning of the poem, is not placed in quotation marks.

Once again, the importance of taking careful notes cannot be underestimated. Be extremely careful when you take your notes so as to avoid the possibility of inadvertently committing plagiarism.

The Note Card Method

There are many possible ways to take notes from source materials. Some people keep notes in notebooks or on legal pads; others make photocopies, and then highlight parts as they read and make notes in the margins. Many high school and college writing courses teach students to research term papers using note cards. Teachers might require that their students use this method and turn in their note cards for grading.

The reason teachers encourage students to use note cards is that they are one of the most efficient and organized means of taking notes for a research paper. As with bibliography cards, note cards enable greater flexibility; you can shuffle the cards, organize them in various groupings, and toss out unneeded notes with ease. Writers particularly find using note cards valuable when it comes time to begin writing, as it places all the needed information at their fingertips, neatly organized in one convenient place. It is therefore highly recommended that you use note cards. You may find it somewhat tedious at first, but the benefits will soon become apparent, and the results will show in your paper.

To use note cards, start, as you did with the bibliography cards, by taking these notes on index cards. You'll probably want to use bigger cards than the ones for bibliography cards so that you have enough room to write your notes (such as 4x6 rather than 3x5). On each card, you will write down one piece of information from a particular source. There is no set format for a note card, as long as you include the necessary information (unless your instructor requires you to do them a certain way, in which case you should follow his or her guidelines).

Before you take notes on any source make sure that you have a complete bibliography card. As these cards will already have all the bibliographic information from the source, you will not have to keep rewriting it on each note card, but can simply cross-reference the cards.

In the top left-hand corner of the card, copy down the last name of the author of the source. If you are using more than one source by a particular author, you should write down the author's last name and a key word or words from the title of that particular source. This will enable you to distinguish between notes taken from different titles. Although not necessary, you might want to do this on all your note cards. This will ensure that you do not forget which source the note came from should you eventually use another source by the same author.

In the top right-hand corner, write down the page number of the outside source from which you are taking notes. Keep very careful track of page numbers in your notes. If you are copying down a quotation that begins on

Jot down your own thoughts and ideas about the subject — again, preferably on note cards.

one page and ends on the next, mark the exact point in the quotation where the next page begins. If you then only include part of the quotation in your paper, you will know which page to attribute it to in your documentation.

Use the remaining lines on the card to take down your notes. If you are copying down a quotation, remember to put it in quotation marks. Also, remember to copy the quotation exactly as it appears in the original source and to note any page breaks. If you are paraphrasing, make certain you rephrase the passage completely in your own words. To further ensure you clearly distinguish between quotations and paraphrases, it is a good idea to write either "QUOTATION" or "PARAPHRASE" at the top of the card in big, bold letters.

Each card should focus upon a *single, specific idea*. Copying lengthy quotations and paraphrasing large chunks of the source takes away the flexibility that making note cards allows you in the first place. Try to confine each card to a single point.

Although not necessary, you might want to use the back of the card to make some of your own notes. While you are conducting research, your mind will be at work on the paper, and you will begin to conceive of various points to make in your paper. Unfortunately, these ideas can often get lost in the onslaught of information you are taking in.

SAMPLE NOTE CARD

Stevens, <u>Shakespeare</u>   p. 42
   Productions of Shakespeare in the 1990s change the scene or time period. Sometimes the change is positive and adds something, but at others it only makes things confusing.
    (PARAPHRASE)

You should therefore write things down as they occur to you, and the note cards are the perfect place to do so.

Take Notes on Your Ideas Too

Regardless of whether or not you are required to conduct research, the heart of the essay should be your own ideas. When no outside sources are included, the assumption is made that the entire essay represents your own thoughts and ideas about the subject. However, even when the essay includes other sources, they should only serve to strengthen and support your ideas.

Whether or not you are conducting research, you should take the time to jot down your ideas before you actually begin writing the essay. In the course of researching and/or

SAMPLE NOTE CARD LISTING THE WRITER'S OWN IDEAS

MY IDEA FOR ESSAY

Cycles and Repetitions in O'Neill's
LONG DAY'S JOURNEY INTO NIGHT

There are lots of images that are repeated throughout LDJ.

- family mealtimes
- cycle of time; one day after another (implied in the title)
- drinking from the bottle then filling with water
- men leaving Mary alone on stage

thinking about your topic, you should have developed certain ideas about the topic and have a sense of the major points you want to make. However, these ideas are still in your head, where they are probably all mixed together. In order to be a compelling, powerful essay, these ideas need to be organized in a logical manner. You first need to get all of your ideas out on paper so you can then examine them and plan a strategic way to address them in the essay. Additionally, the process of writing is akin to brainstorming; as you write about one particular idea or point, you'll probably find yourself conceiving of many additional ones.

Take some time to sit at a computer or with pen and paper and write down any ideas or thoughts you have regarding your chosen topic. You don't need to worry about things such as grammar, spelling, format, or structure; you don't even have to write in complete sentences if you don't want to. Just sit down and write anything that comes to mind in relation to the topic. You can then refer to these notes — along with any notes from additional sources if this is a research paper — as you organize and write your essay.

When you are finished jotting down your ideas, you may want to read over them and transfer the major points onto note cards. That way you can play around with how you organize them and also integrate them with the note cards from outside sources.

Organizing Your Notes

Making a Plan: Outlining

If you're trying to get somewhere you've never been before without a map, chances are you'll get lost. The same holds true for writing your essay. Many writers make the mistake of doing research and then plunging headfirst into the writing process. Often, these papers lack focus, fail to make points effectively, and are generally difficult to read. The truth is if you do not have a plan, writing the paper will be more difficult. It takes enormous energy to write off the top of your head, and you'll probably wind up staring at a blank sheet of paper not knowing where to even begin. As with taking a trip, it's much easier when you know both where you've come from and exactly where you're going.

The most effective way to do this is by making a rough outline. An outline is simply a list of the main points you intend to make in your paper, put in the approximate order in which you plan to address them.

You're probably thinking to yourself, When am I going to write this thing already? While doing an outline may seem tiresome, it is not a meaningless exercise. It will make the process of writing the paper much easier for you. Everything will be in one place and clearly organized. Instead of shuffling through notes and papers, you'll be free to concentrate on writing brilliantly.

The outline will also enable you to plan a strategy, helping you to order your points in such a way as to instill them with more impact and power. By definition, strategy is something that is planned in advance. When a general plans an attack, he does it before the fight begins, not when he's already feeling the heat of battle and it's too late to make a difference. By the same token, strategy cannot develop randomly when you are in the midst of writing. The time to plot out your strategy is before you begin writing — with an outline.

You do not, however, have to wait until you have completed your research to begin designing an outline. You can make a working outline even while you are still conducting research. This will help you keep track of all the information you are compiling and ensure that no great ideas slip through the cracks. Like your working bibliography, the working outline will develop as you conduct research, eventually becoming a final outline. As it is primarily for your own benefit, you can revise the working outline as often as you like. (Occasionally, instructors will require that students submit working outlines, in which case you will have to write one that is a bit more formal than one you would write just for yourself. You can use the same format as for a final outline.)

Before constructing the final outline, you should have a pretty strong sense of what you intend to say in the paper, including several main points you plan on making to prove your argument. This will come naturally out of the research process. Somewhere in the back of your mind, you've been thinking about your thesis statement and the paper all along; you've been making connections between different sources you've read and relating them to your own understanding of the material. If you don't have many ideas at this point, you probably need to do more research or maybe even change your thesis. Only when you believe you have enough material for the paper — enough to prove the thesis beyond a shadow of a doubt — will you be ready to make a final outline and then begin writing.

The outline, in effect, is the skeleton of the actual paper. So you need to have an understanding of the structure of a research paper before you design your outline. We will examine the paper structure in the next chapter. Read both this chapter and the next before making your outline.

Working with the Note Cards

The first step in creating the outline is to re-examine your notes. After you feel you've taken enough notes, take all of the cards and skim through them.

Sorting through the note cards is somewhat of a weeding-out process. As you read through the cards, evaluate how effective they might be in your paper, and whether they are even necessary for your paper. Decide whether each note does in fact relate to your thesis. If not, feel free to toss it aside. *Everything in the paper has to support the thesis statement.* Everything else just adds clutter to your paper, distracting the reader from your argument and thereby taking away from its overall impact.

The majority of the notes you have taken will probably not apply to your thesis statement, but that's okay. You should have plenty of material left. And by carefully evaluating the notes, you ensure that only the most powerful material remains. You are merely picking the gems out of a substantial lode of raw materials. One of the qualities that separates a good writer from a mediocre one is knowing not only what to put in, but what to leave out.

It might feel painful to throw away material; you may wonder why you made all that effort in the first place. Rest assured that all that note taking has helped make you an expert in your field, and your paper will show it.

As you read through the note cards, begin to group those cards that seem to belong together. You can start by separating them into the most general categories, spreading them out in piles around the room. Try to conceive of a key word or words to describe each category. For example, if you are writing a paper about "Hamlet and Madness," you might have categories such as "The Ghost," "Hamlet and Ophelia," and "Hamlet's Theatricality." Put the category name at the top of each card in that pile. That way you won't have to worry if the cards become mixed up or further separated.

Since each note card is supposed to focus upon a single idea, you should be able to group the cards into distinct categories. If a card seems to belong in more than one category, place it in the one that seems most applicable. You may, though, want to note the other categories in which it might be used in case you later decide to move it.

In organizing the cards into categories, you have, in effect, been organizing the paper. These categories will be similar to the main sections of your outline and your paper. When you write, you will probably want to narrow down further, removing cards or even whole categories. For now, however, you have a general sense of the material you have at your disposal. Your paper is beginning to take shape.

Within each category, you can then subdivide into smaller sections. These subcategories contribute to and help support the various major points in the paper. These notes might eventually become specific paragraphs or parts of paragraphs in your paper.

Standard Outline Format

The outline simply lists the major points of the essay, and beneath the major points, the subpoints and sub-subpoints that are a part of each. Using Roman numerals, capital letters, lowercase letters, and numbers, the outline orders the various categories so that the smaller subpoints are always listed beneath the more general ones to which they apply. As subpoints become more removed from the major point, they are indented more in the outline. Whenever two points are aligned, meaning they are indented equally, they carry approximately the same weight in the overall paper.

The major points are listed by Roman numeral. Subpoints of these major categories are then listed beneath them by capital letter, and sub-subpoints beneath them by number. You can continue listing further subpoints by using lowercase letters, and numbers and letters in parentheses.

> This is a sketch of the overall ordering of an outline:
>
> I. MAJOR POINT ONE
>   A. Subpoint of I.
>   1. Subpoint of A. (Sub-subpoint of I.)
>   2. Subpoint of A. (Sub-subpoint of I.)
>   B. Subpoint of I.
>
> II. MAJOR POINT TWO

In the sample above, Roman numeral I refers to some major point in the paper. Both A and B, indented equally beneath Roman numeral I, are both subpoints of I. Since A comes first, it is probably a bit more important or extensive than B. Beneath A, there are two subpoints that refer to or support A. By extension, they refer to Roman numeral I as well.

Here's an example of how an actual outline might look. This one is for part of a paper on "Hamlet and Madness":

I. Introduction
II. Hamlet as an actor
   A. Hamlet's theatricality
      1. Makes speech to the players
      2. Engineers theatrical "scenes"
         a. The Mousetrap production
         b. Rosencrantz and Guildenstern's death
   B. Hamlet "plays" mad
      1. Plans to put on an "antic disposition"
      2. Urges Ophelia, "Get thee to a nunnery."

Do you see how each subpoint is a subset of the one above it, which is in turn a subset of the one above it?

In general, you can continue adding points and subpoints as long as you like by continuing to indent and change the style of classification (from number to letter, from uppercase to lowercase).

There are two kinds of formal outlines: the topic outline and the sentence outline. A topic outline lists the various points in phrases of just a few key words, such as in the sample outline on Hamlet. It is clean, concise, and to the point, and it allows a great degree of freedom and flexibility.

A sentence outline, as its name implies, lists various points using complete, grammatically correct sentences. You will want to use a sentence outline primarily when someone else is to read it, as it makes it easier for the other person to follow your line of thinking. If you are required to submit an outline for your class, you should ask your instructor for guidelines as to the format and style.

If you are making the outline just for yourself, you need not worry about strict formats; do whatever makes the most sense to you. As long as you can distinguish between the major points, subpoints, and sub-subpoints, you can list the various categories however you like.

Designing Your Rough Outline

After going through your notes, you'll be sitting with several piles of note cards spread out in the room, made up of the general categories and smaller subcategories within them. Believe it or not, that's your outline. These piles simply become listings of points and subpoints in the outline. The only thing you need to do is decide what order to put the categories in.

The standard research paper is divided into three parts, the *introduction*, *body*, and *conclusion* (we'll discuss this in detail in the next chapter). Roman numeral I on your outline will always be the introduction. The last Roman numeral will always be the conclusion. Underneath the Roman numeral for the introduction, write out your thesis statement, as this is where it will go in the paper. You don't necessarily have to put in anything else right now, unless you have an idea of what you want to say in the introduction.

Everything between the introduction and conclusion is known as the body of the paper. It is here that you will include all of the evidence, from your research and your own ideas, that supports the thesis statement. Your general category headings from your note cards will be listed by Roman numerals on the outline. The cards within those categories will then be listed as subpoints of the larger ones, using letters and numbers.

Deciding what order to place the categories and subcategories in is not that easy; you can't simply throw them in the air and list them in whatever order they land. In the next chapter, we'll examine some ways of organizing the body of the paper. Reading that chapter will help you to organize your outline as well.

In general, though, there are two basic organizing principles you need to keep in mind:

1. Logic. When organizing the outline, make certain that you order the points in a logical fashion. You want one point clearly to lead to the next, so that the reader will be able to follow your argument without having to fill in any gaps that have been left unexplained.

Keeping logic in mind, certain categories will have to follow others and will, in effect, order themselves. For example, if you are going to contradict a particular theory, you first need to describe the theory before giving your evidence against it or it wouldn't make any sense. After reading over the note cards and organizing them into categories, you probably already have some idea which ones will have to be described earlier in the paper in order for later ones to make sense.

There are many ways to organize a paper. The overall governing organizational principle, though, is logic. For example, if you are writing a historical term paper, it may make the most sense to order your facts chronologically, particularly if you are trying to establish a domino-like momentum to the events. On the other hand, when analyzing a work of literature, it is not necessary that you discuss events in the plot in chronological order. In this case, you are analyzing the work as a whole, and you can freely discuss whatever events in the plot relate to the point you are trying to make.

Examine your groupings of note cards and see if you can determine which ones must logically go together or follow one another. You probably won't have the entire outline completed, and you may not know yet where to place certain categories. However, you will have gotten a start on ordering your paper.

2. Strategy. Although the most important organizing principle to follow is ensuring the logical order of your points, at the same time, you want to organize your points so that they will be especially powerful in building your case. You therefore need to decide what kind of strategy to use.

Before lawyers go to court, they carefully prepare how they intend to present their evidence, the order they plan to call up witnesses, and what line of questioning they will follow. They do all of this with some kind of plan in mind that will help their case. For example, there's a reason why the surprise witness is always called in last, creating a hush over the spectators. Having a surprise witness come last is a strategic decision that has great dramatic impact. In writing your paper, you need to think along similar crafty, strategic lines.

Evaluate your different pieces of evidence. Some will no doubt be more powerful than others; these are your star witnesses. With this in mind, consider how to order these pieces of evidence so that they make the most persuasive argument and pack the most punch. Strategically, you may want to build up to your strongest points so as to leave your reader with these ideas foremost in mind, absolutely convinced of your argument. At the same time, though, you won't want to start with your weakest points either, giving the reader a lukewarm first impression.

Strategy is a personal decision. Each writer will have his or her own favorite strategic devices, and each paper will have its own strategic method behind it. You need to consider for yourself the overall effect you want to create in the paper and the way you want to go about achieving it.

Read through your note cards and throw out any that don't apply to the thesis. Organize the remaining cards into categories and subcategories.

Fine-Tuning the Outline

When trying to put your various groupings of note cards into an order for the outline, it may be easier for you to begin by organizing the smaller subcategories within each category. As all of these subcategories are closely related to one another, logic patterns will probably be more evident to you. Organizing the larger categories — the main points of the paper — is a bit more difficult, as this is where you have a lot more choice and will need to think strategically.

Remember, the outline is not written in stone. When you are in the rhythm of writing the paper, you may find that a certain point works much better in a different place than you originally planned. That's okay. You can veer from the path a bit, but you'll still be heading in the same direction that you've plotted out beforehand.

Try to make the outline as detailed as possible. The more specific details you put into the outline, the easier it will be to do your paper. Beneath the categories on the outline, you can list various sources (and even page numbers of sources) that you plan to discuss in relation to the category. You might even write out specific quotations that you intend to introduce at that point in the paper.

The Three-Part Essay Structure

*T*here are various formats for organizing an essay. However, the standard three-part essay is an effective, clear, basic approach and is therefore recommended here. This chapter will describe the elements of this paper format. You don't need to worry about starting to write the essay just yet; that comes in the next chapter. For now, simply read this section to gain a sense of the overall structure of this kind of essay. You can then start writing based on what you read here.

The standard three-part essay structure is similar to a court proceeding. In a trial, the lawyer first makes opening remarks, briefly stating for the judge or jury the exact status of his or her case (such as how the client pleads) and how, through the course of the proceedings, he or she intends to prove it. Next, the lawyer spends the bulk of the legal proceeding carefully and methodically presenting evidence that supports the case. Finally, when finished presenting evidence, the lawyer will give a summation, quickly recapping the main points that have proven the case.

A standard paper is structured in much the same way as a legal proceeding, with three distinct parts that roughly correspond to the parts of a trial and fulfill the same purpose. They're called the *introduction*, the *body* and the *conclusion*.

The Introduction

Like the lawyer's opening statement, the introduction of the paper is where you lay out your argument for the judge, the reader of your essay. Most introductions will only be one paragraph, although in bigger projects (more than twenty pages) it might be somewhat longer. As in a trial, you do not want to spend the bulk of the proceeding just setting up your argument; you want to spend it actually arguing. By being succinct, the introduction will have much more impact.

You want the introduction to draw your reader into your argument right from the beginning. It's somewhat like a movie preview; you are going to give your audience a short taste of what's to come, but not the whole story. You want your reader to be enticed, immediately interested in what you have to say, and curious about how you are going to say it. The introduction should grab onto the reader, and pull him or her into the body of the paper.

As it summarizes the gist of your argument, your thesis statement will naturally be an important part of the introduction. But it can't be an introduction on its own. In most cases the thesis statement will only be one sentence, certainly too short to make an impressive introduction.

Moreover, as we have seen, a thesis statement is very specific and often represents a different or unusual view of the material. If you simply write out your thesis statement at the top of the paper without elaborating on it, you are probably going to confuse or even annoy the reader. You therefore need to set it up before introducing the thesis to your reader.

The standard form of the introduction is structured to set up the thesis statement. The last sentence of the introduction will be the thesis statement, enabling you to use the entire paragraph to set the stage. The introductory paragraph is therefore a kind of introduction to your thesis statement, beginning in a general manner, slowly easing the reader into your argument. You want the bulk of the introduction to establish the general arena from which your thesis emerges and within which you will be presenting your argument in the paper.

The first sentence of the introduction — the first sentence of your entire paper — is your reader's first taste of the topic and your point of view. Make certain that you make a good first impression. It should be well-written, interesting, and, most importantly, give the reader some idea of what the paper is going to be about.

The rest of the introduction bridges this first general statement to the thesis statement. After your opening line, each subsequent sentence will be literally and figuratively one step closer to the thesis statement. By the time the reader comes to your thesis statement, he or she should have a strong sense of the kind of paper this is going to be, what issues and topics it will be addressing, and the writer's take on them.

Before it was time to write the introduction, you only needed an idea of what your thesis statement would say. Now, you will have to decide upon the exact wording. When you write the thesis statement in your introduction, it is the first and possibly the only place in which you will spell it out for your reader. You therefore need to be extremely careful about the wording of your thesis statement in the introduction. You want to phrase it so that it will not be at all ambiguous. It does not have to be fancy, flashy, or wordy; the power of the idea should be enough to impress your reader.

Like the thesis statement, the introduction should come from you. In general, this is not the place to begin introducing your secondary sources. The secondary sources, as we will see, will be presented in the body of the paper to support whatever argument you initially set up in the introduction. It would not make sense to present evidence without first stating what argument you are trying to make. Moreover, you want the reader to be immediately impressed by the power of your own voice, the depth of your understanding of the topic and the strength of your own ideas.

This is an example of a standard, straightforward introduction:

> In Shakespeare's plays, madness and tragedy seem to go hand in hand. All of his great tragic figures, including Macbeth and Lady Macbeth, Othello, Hamlet, and

King Lear, grapple with madness in some form or other. To a large extent, their insanity illuminates aspects of their character, as Shakespeare uses it to convey the personal torment and anguish that these characters experience in the wake of their tragic circumstances. However, Shakespeare uses insanity not only to point out a tragic character's personal torment, but also to convey his or her alienation from the larger social structure.

The above introduction begins with a generalized statement that lets the reader know the topic, in this case, madness in Shakespeare's tragedies. It then narrows down to the thesis statement, laying out a specific point of view of the topic.

There are several variations on this standard format. Although the introduction is generally not the place in which to introduce secondary sources, one effective format does draw on the research you have conducted. In this variation of the standard introduction, you begin by summarizing a trend in the critical material and research on your subject. You then set up how your thesis either conforms to or differs from this body of material.

When you write this kind of introduction, you do not specify individual sources, but write a general summation of a body of sources. Just make certain that your summation is accurate, that it does in fact summarize a substantial portion of the secondary material. (To ensure that you do not leave yourself open to attack on this point, you should include a bibliographic note — a footnote at the bottom of the page listing several secondary sources that support your statement.)

Here is an example of this format:

> Many critics, writing in the wake of Freud, have primarily addressed the question of Hamlet's sanity. A body of scholarly material is devoted to answering the question of whether or not Hamlet, in playing mad, actually goes mad. However, by focusing all discussion of the play on Hamlet's individual psyche, critics have ignored the larger social setting that Shakespeare so carefully establishes. The social setting and Hamlet's psyche are intricately interwoven, as Shakespeare uses madness to indicate Hamlet's alienated status within the larger society of the play.

This introduction is much more centered on the scholarly discussion of the play. The first sentences not only let the reader know that this will be a paper about Hamlet and madness, but that it will be a highly analytical one, centered in criticism and research. The writer begins by summarizing a critical trend, without going into too much specific detail about it. (A bibliographic note would list several essays that support this assertion.) After presenting this summation of a critical trend, the writer then discusses what he or she sees as the problem with this viewpoint, and finally presents the thesis statement, which counters it.

Similarly, if your entire argument hinges upon some influential theory, book, essay, or article, or the ideas of a particular researcher or critic, then you will probably want to mention that particular source in your introduction. However, you must still follow the same conventions of a standard introduction. The influential source you describe serves as the general arena out of which your thesis statement emerges. In the introduction, you describe the gist of this particular secondary source in general terms, and then establish how your argument either agrees with or differs from it. You then elaborate more on the specifics of the source later in your paper.

The Body

The bulk of your paper is made up of the body; it's where you will at last argue your case in detail. After having conducted research and given your topic great thought, you should have several points you would like to make to prove your thesis. In the body, you will present these ideas.

The most important thing to keep in mind is that e*very bit of information you include in the body should relate to the thesis, and you must spell out exactly how it does*. Remember that the reader cannot see inside your head. You must therefore explain all of your points very carefully, making it crystal clear for the reader what they mean and how they tie into and support your overall argument.

Introducing Evidence

Merely listing your ideas is not enough to prove your thesis conclusively. This is why you need to bring in supporting evidence from your primary and secondary sources, as they lend greater credence to your ideas. This does not mean, however, that these outside sources replace your own ideas. You are bringing them in to support your ideas, not to overwhelm them.

Each time you quote or paraphrase from an outside source, you need to include a citation that documents the source's origin. This is done according to a standard format so it will be clear to anyone reading your paper what ideas come from outside sources. Make certain you read the chapter on citing sources which discusses how to do this properly.

If your paper is centered upon some primary source — meaning that you are mainly analyzing a particular work or works — it is extremely important that you draw upon the primary source extensively in your paper. Facts drawn directly from the primary source are the strongest kinds of evidence you have at your disposal. As they have not been translated through another person's eyes, they are a much more valid, and therefore potent, form of evidence. You should therefore try to quote from a primary source often and in detail. Be sure to cite the source, including a page number.

In many essays, especially research papers, you'll also need to include material drawn from your secondary sources. You must demonstrate your knowledge of the research that has been conducted by various experts in the field. These established researchers and writers can help lend support to your interpretation of the text. They are not irrefutable, however, and you may also counter what they say, as long as you have strong evidence supporting your view.

Direction of the Body

The body should not randomly bring up points and then drop them haphazardly. Instead, it should have an overall direction, with the various points building on one another and propelling the paper forward. This is where strategic planning comes into play, which you can try to map out in your outline.

There are various ways to organize the paper's body, and you should consider one that best serves your purposes. One common method is to begin your discussion in broad, general terms, laying a solid groundwork for more sophisticated points to come. After establishing the main, less refutable points, you then can become progressively more specific and complex in your discussion. It is like building a house; you first lay out a sturdy foundation, and them move on to the more intricate frame.

Another approach is to establish various specific points in the beginning stages of the paper and then tie them into broader, more theoretical schemes in the latter parts.

These are only two common means of organizing the overall arc of the body, but there are many others, and you may find one more suitable to you. Your primary concern should be that the paper flows smoothly, with one idea logically leading to the next. If you organize your paper with this in mind, the body will have a momentum that emerges on its own.

Ways of Introducing Information

Within the body, there are many ways to introduce and discuss material. Alternating the ways you present your ideas and evidence adds variety to the paper, making it more interesting to read.

Among the many techniques you may use are the following suggestions, which you can use in any combination:

Description.   This kind of writing features very detailed, highly descriptive language that essentially recreates an object, work, or event, but without making any kind of critical evaluation.

Certain papers, sometimes called descriptive papers, are almost entirely devoted to description. All papers, however, will have parts in which the writer describes something. For example, if you were to write a paper about a play, such as *Hamlet*, you might choose to describe certain scenes that support your thesis. Similarly, if you were writing a paper on the Civil War, you might include a paragraph in which you describe various modes of combat during the war. These passages help make the paper more colorful, dramatic, and interesting.

However, even when you are describing something in your paper, you still must make certain it relates to the thesis and that your reader will see the connection. You cannot randomly describe things without making the connection clear; this will distract the reader from your argument.

There is an important distinction between description and summary. Description, in elaborating upon a particular work or object, enhances the reader's view of it, and thereby lends additional support to your argument. You use it to highlight a particular side or point of view of the work or object. Summarization, on the other hand, is almost always unnecessary in a paper, as your reader is

You should be careful not to use too many descriptive passages, (unless, of course, your assignment is to write a descriptive paper).

probably already familiar with the material and, if not, can certainly find out about it for him or herself.

For example, if you are writing for an English teacher, you need not summarize the plot of *Hamlet* as you can assume the teacher already knows it. You might, though, want to describe a specific scene in order to highlight a particular aspect of it that relates to your argument. If you are discussing the question of Hamlet's sanity, for example, you might describe the scene in which he confronts Polonius as a means of establishing how Hamlet behaves in various situations.

As this example indicates, most descriptive passages work best together with some form of evaluation or analysis that puts the description into perspective and relates it to the overall argument.

Description may help make your argument more effective, but it won't prove your argument on its own. You do not want to tie up the body of the paper with descriptions, when you should instead be discussing your research and your ideas that will prove your argument. You can describe something in anywhere from a few words to a paragraph. If it takes longer than a paragraph, chances are it is becoming too extensive and is not all that necessary.

In short, do not include a description unless it will add fuel to your fire.

Presentation and Definition.   Closely related to description, the presentation or definition of material is another means of including information in the paper. You introduce and define, usually in one or two lines, a particular source or piece of information, without necessarily elaborating upon it. For example, if you are writing a paper about the Civil War, you might include one paragraph in which you present the various perspectives from which the war has been analyzed.

Critical Argument, Evaluation, and Analysis.   Most writing in research papers will be of this type, in which you not only introduce material, but proceed to evaluate it from a critical perspective. You do so to establish the information as valid and relevant to your argument, or, if it contradicts your argument, to counter it.

All writing is a form of interpretation, and therefore open to criticism and evaluation from differing perspectives. When you write your paper, you want to evaluate the material for your reader in a way that highlights how it supports your argument. You approach the source material from the perspective of an expert, evaluating it with the benefit of your substantial background knowledge and intimate understanding of the material which you have attained in the process of doing the research. If you do this in a convincing manner, your reader will not question your interpretation or the validity of your argument. In short, you want your reader to buy into your argument without question.

You especially will want to approach primary sources — those texts that are the focus of the paper — in a critical fashion. The essence of most papers is the writer's particular interpretation of some primary source or sources. You therefore want to draw out the parts of the primary source that agree with your interpretation and criticize or argue against those that disagree.

At the same time, you want to approach your secondary sources in a critical fashion. As you have been taking notes, you have already begun evaluating the various sources and determining their validity and the extent to which they might support your argument. When you now introduce information from these secondary sources in the body of the paper, you can indicate to the reader your critical evaluation of them. For example, you may mention certain theories, studies, or interpretations that you disagree with. You can then proceed to describe why you disagree with these views, using other sources to prove your point.

Much of the body might also be devoted to analyzing a specific passage, during which you either quote or paraphrase an entire passage, and then discuss and interpret it in a critical fashion. When you analyze material, always try to do so in detail, referring to specific aspects of it.

Compare/Contrast. This is a particular type of critical argument that can be especially powerful in helping you prove your case. Very simply, you introduce several pieces of information together (primary or secondary sources or excerpts from them), and evaluate them against one another. You then indicate which ideas or sources are comparatively stronger than others, and submit these principles in support of your thesis.

Although a teacher will sometimes ask students to write personal responses, this kind of writing has traditionally been frowned upon in the research paper. However, many schools are now encouraging students to incorporate personal narrative into their papers.

Differing Points of View.   This is another means of critical argument that is also extremely effective. You introduce one mode of interpretation, a particular theory or study, for example, and then hypothesize in the paper how this interpretation might change if approached from a different point of view:

> Many critics have argued that *Hamlet* is a play about a tormented individual. However, it might also be thought of as a play about a tormented society.

You can then discuss how this different perspective sheds new light on the topic and use it in support of your overall argument.

Personal Response.   Personal response is a kind of writing in which the writer expresses intimate thoughts, feelings, and reactions about a particular subject or brings in personal experiences to reflect upon it. Of course, all writing is in some form or another a writer's personal response. But most papers are written from an objective standpoint, meaning that the writer is somewhat removed from the material and lets the information and sources stand on their own. In a personal response, on the other hand, the writer is an active presence, and the reader is consciously aware of the writer's voice. This is primarily achieved through the use of first person narrative ("I think," "I feel," etc.).

The Conclusion

The paper begins with an introduction in which you make a claim — your thesis statement — and promise to prove your case to your reader. The body of the paper is then spent presenting evidence to achieve this goal. Ultimately, all of this evidence leads right back to the thesis statement, but now seen from a very different perspective than in the introduction.

After reading the body and all the evidence you have presented, the reader should now view your thesis statement not as conjecture, but as proven fact. And that's exactly what you are going to tell the reader in your conclusion. Although it is never couched in these explicit terms, all conclusions have the same underlying meaning and say essentially the same thing: I have successfully proven what I said I was going to in my introduction.

The conclusion is therefore a kind of mirror image of your introduction — but one that stresses the fact that the thesis has now been proven. Like the introduction, the conclusion for most term papers need only be one paragraph (unless it is a particularly long paper of more than fifteen to twenty pages). And also similar to the introduction, the conclusion should come from you and be primarily dominated by your voice and ideas. This is not a place to quote or paraphrase extensively from secondary sources.

While the introduction is the first taste of your paper, your conclusion is the last. You therefore want to end with a bang, with some of your most powerful writing, leaving the reader impressed with your expertise and absolutely convinced of the validity of your argument.

The conclusion should therefore again include the thesis statement in some form or other, but affirm that it has been conclusively proven. The standard way to accomplish this, one that many instructors advise their students to use, is to invert the structure of the introduction. You begin by restating the thesis statement, reworded a bit to emphasize that it is now proven, and then expand upon it until you end with a broad, general statement. As in a lawyer's closing summation, you should also try to recap some of the major points you have made in your paper that have helped establish your argument.

This example of this standard kind of conclusion is from the paper on "Madness in Shakespeare." Compare it to the sample introduction presented earlier from the same paper:

> Shakespeare's tragic figures then are removed from the larger societies he depicts in the plays, and he dramatically emphasizes this alienation, as we have seen, through madness. The madness that so many of his tragic figures display is not only the result of their tragic circumstances, but in a larger sense, symptomatic of it. Shakespeare therefore seems to use madness for a twofold purpose: to indicate something about the nature of the tragic character, but also to establish something about the individual's role in society.

This is a standard form of a conclusion. As with the introduction, there are many other ways to approach it. Many writers choose to introduce some new point or question in the conclusion that emerges from the thesis. After establishing the validity of the thesis, they then address its consequences or implications.

Depending on the flexibility and freedom your instructor allows you, you can try to be bold and creative in the conclusion, just as you may in the introduction. However, the same rule applies: The conclusion must bring the paper to a close and affirm that the thesis has been proven.

A Final Word on Structure

The three-part paper structure that we have examined here is one found in most term papers. However, it is not a hard and fast law that this format be used. As you read academic books and articles, you will find that some writers follow it and others do not. Many academic institutions are currently questioning the relevance of teaching this standard structure.

Learning about this structure is valuable, however, because it is particularly effective. It ensures that the paper remains focused upon a main idea (the thesis statement), and that it is presented in a straightforward and logical fashion. Understanding and following this structure will probably help you to write powerful and persuasive papers, especially when you are first learning how to write. Once you are familiar with and comfortable writing the standard structure, you will then get a sense of how you might stray from it but still write strong and compelling papers.

Writing and Revising the Essay

Writing in Stages

One of the hardest aspects of writing an essay is getting started. Even after all the work and research you've done, it can be very intimidating to sit down and start writing. Part of the difficulty comes from the way we tend to view writing. We don't think of how much writing is a process, and only value the finished product, which is supposed to be flawless. That way of thinking places tremendous pressure on you the first time you try to write; you think it needs to be perfect, so you freeze up with panic, afraid to commit yourself to a single word on paper.

Good writing takes time and effort to produce. You can't expect to zip off the perfect essay on the first try, and, in fact, you shouldn't even attempt it. Instead, it's better to write in several stages, each time making changes and improvements. That way you won't feel the pressure to produce perfection the first time you sit down to write.

The First Draft

Correct grammar and spelling are important parts of an essay because they help make it understandable and readable. However, you don't necessarily have to concern yourself with this in your first draft. At this point, the most important task is to get all of your ideas on paper and integrate notes from other sources. This eliminates a great deal of the stress about writing; you don't have to think about the "rules" at first and can simply concentrate on conveying your ideas.

Start at the beginning of the rough outline and simply start writing. Do your best to explain each of the points you've listed. As you need to, refer to your note cards and include quotations or paraphrases from other sources. Make sure you include citations for each sentence you include with information from another source (see the chapter on citing sources). Keep on writing until you've reached the end of the rough outline. Don't stop to go back or make changes. If you hit a road block, a point when you freeze and don't know how to proceed, mark the place with an X and move on to another point. You can go back later and work on the trouble spot.

This first draft will be extremely rough; the writing will probably be choppy and it will be difficult to read. But that's okay. It's only the first draft and you are the only one who has to see it. Writing this draft provides you with the raw material for your essay; you can then take the time to work on it and refine it until it is a real gem. That's something you just can't do with only a blank sheet of paper.

Tips on Writing an Introduction and Conclusion

As you draft your introduction, remember that the way you approach your topic in the introduction sets up certain expectations for your reader about the rest of the paper. Try to take into consideration the kind of effect you want to produce in the paper as a whole and how you can set it up in the introduction. Do you want to be descriptive, analytical, or critical? Do you want to describe or challenge a particular trend or theory? Do you want to challenge or intrigue the reader? The tone and style of the language you use will help you to produce the desired effect.

At first, you may want to write very standard introductions. As you become more comfortable with writing papers, you will feel more confident being creative and even daring in the introduction. No matter how you write the introduction, make certain that it establishes the paper's topic and that it clearly presents the thesis.

The introduction should feature some of the strongest writing in your paper. This means it will take somewhat more thought and effort. Many writers try to begin at the beginning and, faced with the pressure of writing a brilliant introduction, find themselves frozen. As long as you have a thesis statement, you can skip the introduction, for now, and begin writing the rest of the paper first. After designing your outline, you're probably more than ready to start writing the body of the paper, so it will be an easier place to begin. Once you have written a part or even all of the body, you will then have a better idea of what you want to say in your introduction. You can then go back to the beginning.

Just because the introduction comes first in your paper does not mean that you necessarily have to write it first.

The same thinking largely holds true for the conclusion. You'll want this paragraph to be powerful, assertive, and very well-written. Try also to make it somewhat different from the introduction, even though it will make the same general points. You can hold off on writing the conclusion until after you've revised the body several times; when the body comes close to being final, you'll feel more confident about building on it in your conclusion.

Tips on Drafting the Body

There are many ways to present material and make your points in the body, but they need not be distinguished from one another or labeled as they were in the previous chapter. You already know all the ways to make a convincing argument. Whenever you try to convince someone of your viewpoint in conversation, you make use of the same techniques that you would on paper.

As you concentrate upon ways to prove your thesis, you should naturally be able to come up with convincing arguments. One of the reasons the example of a lawyer arguing a case in court is useful is because a lawyer's arguments are done orally and therefore seem somewhat more familiar and less restricted than written arguments. But both written and oral arguments follow the same principles of logic.

It may therefore help you to "talk" through your ideas in your head or even out loud. If you were to try to explain your thesis to a friend, what would you say? How would you describe or introduce the source material to convince your friend? You may even want to talk through your paper with a friend. Be conscious of how you phrase things, the kinds of arguments you make, and the logic behind them. Whatever you say can be written down.

In general, there are three important components of a well-written body to keep in mind:

Material Clearly Relates to Thesis Statement.   The most important thing to keep in mind when writing the body is that every bit of information you include should relate to the thesis and you must spell out exactly how it does. If something doesn't relate to the thesis, get rid of it; it's only clouding up your argument and detracting from its power.

It's All Down on Paper.   You are so closely tied to your ideas that you can understand them without confusion, no matter how they are written down on paper. Because it all makes sense to you, you may think you have fully explained a point or idea, when in fact you haven't done so in a manner that someone else can read and understand. The reader cannot see inside your head. You must therefore explain all your points carefully, making it clear to the reader what they mean and how they support or tie into your overall argument. Don't worry that you are over-explaining your points and ideas. It may seem that way to you, but a reader will need a detailed explanation in order to see your points as clearly as you do.

It Flows Smoothly.   As the writer of the essay, it's your job to act as the guide for the reader. As you ease the reader through the complexities of your argument, journeying from one point to the next, you want to follow as smooth a path as possible so that by the end of the essay the reader won't feel disoriented. At times, you need to make it clear exactly where the essay is heading or summarize what has already been demonstrated. You also don't want the paper to be choppy or difficult to read. Instead, one idea or point should flow smoothly into the next.

Reading and Revising

Once you have completed the first draft, you should go back to the beginning and read it from start to finish. You should try to read the draft from an objective standpoint, as if you are someone else reading your work. Because you are so closely tied to your ideas, it might be difficult at first to be objective about it. Try to think of yourself as an editor going over an article by one of your reporters. As an editor, it's your job to make certain that everyone reading the newspaper will be able to understand the article. You might also try reading it out loud and listen to how it sounds when spoken.

As you read the draft, sit with a pen in your hand and make notes. Try to anticipate specific questions a reader might have about what is on the page and write them down in the margins.

After you've read over the draft and made notes on it, then go back to the beginning and revise it. As you revise,

As you read over your draft, ask yourself questions about what you see on the page:

- Is everything explained fully?
- Will the reader understand everything as it is currently explained?
- Are there any holes or gaps in the argument?
- Are any ideas not fully developed or only partially explained?
- Does one idea flow smoothly into the next?
- What additional information does the reader need to appreciate this point?

include more information that answers those questions a reader might have when reading the essay. You should continue to reread and revise the essay as many times as necessary until you are satisfied with it. Each time you redraft, you make changes to improve the essay.

The first few times you read and rewrite, you should focus on the content — the ideas and points that are explained in the essay. Make certain all your ideas are clearly and fully explained, that nothing is ambiguous or partially stated, and that there are no gaps in the discussion. Examine the overall organization of the essay and make sure that one point flows smoothly and logically into the next. You might try moving sections of the essay around to see if they work more effectively and strategically somewhere else. Verify that everything in the essay supports the thesis statement, and take out anything that detracts from the argument.

In later revisions, you can concentrate less on the content and more on the writing itself. Read through the essay and pay attention to how things are phrased. Work on individual paragraphs and sentences to ensure they are well-written and flow together. Think about ways you might rephrase or reword various sentences to make them clearer or more effective. The chapter Tips for Good Writing offers some suggestions.

Computers to the Rescue

Since revision is such a vital component of writing a strong essay, it is highly recommended that you get in the habit of working on a computer. A computer makes it much easier to make changes and continually rewrite, revise, and rework text. Every time you want to reread a draft, you can simply print out a new clean copy. If you want to revise the structure of the essay, you can simply "cut and paste" sections, moving around information to different places in the essay without having to retype the whole essay.

Owning your own computer is the most convenient way to work on essays. Of course, buying a computer can be expensive, but it is well worth the investment, especially if you will need to write many papers. When buying a computer, consider what your priorities are. What do you plan to use the computer for most? Will the model you are looking at provide you with everything you require? Is it important to you to be able to carry the computer around from place to place? Is it important to you that the computer have enough memory to run many different programs? Do you want to have a

CD-ROM? A color monitor? It might help to do some research before buying a computer. Read some computer magazines to see which models are particularly recommended for certain tasks. Ask around and find out what computers other students are using and whether they would recommend them. If you know someone who is a computer expert, get him or her to go shopping with you.

If you do have financial considerations, don't despair. Computers also range significantly in price. Depending on the options you choose, you may be able to find a computer that fits in your price range. You might also consider buying a used computer. Again, ask around and see if someone you know is interested in selling his or her computer. You might consider placing a classified ad in the school newspaper.

Many schools also offer students special discounts if they purchase computer equipment from the school. Ask at your school bookstore, if there is one, what kind of discount you might get.

If you do not want to buy a computer, you can probably still work on one as you write your essay. Most schools now have computer labs in which students can work on a computer for free. You might have to sign up for time or wait for an available computer, so be sure you plan ahead and give yourself enough time to work on the essay. Many schools also offer classes and seminars on different computer programs so that you can learn how to use them. If you don't know how to use a computer, this is the time to learn and get in the habit of using it for writing essays.

If you do not want to work on a computer, you will need to type your final essay. You don't, however, have to keep typing each time you revise, which would be terribly time consuming. You can do earlier drafts and revisions on paper by hand. Just remember, though, that the final paper will have to be typed so that it is neat and clear for the reader.

Citing Sources and 8
Creating Bibliographies

Giving Credit

Each time you introduce information from an outside source into your paper *you must document exactly where it came from*. You need to do this for *everything* in your paper that comes from a source other than your head — whether it be a quotation, paraphrase, or even an idea or theory. In other words, you must always give credit where credit is due. If you do not, you are committing plagiarism.

As you might imagine, quoting, paraphrasing, and crediting sources within an essay can become quite messy, especially if you aren't consistent about the way you do it. To help make essays readable, standard formats have been developed that designate the proper way to include and credit sources. Standard formats provide consistency within an essay; they ensure that each time you introduce an outside source it is done in the same way and includes the correct documentation. These formats also provide consistency from one essay to the next, so that any reader might pick up any text and see where other sources are incorporated and know exactly what those original sources are.

Any time you quote directly from another source, that is, anytime you include information from another source exactly the way it appears in that original source, you must put it in quotation marks in the essay and include a citation that gives information about which source the quotation comes from. Be extra careful when quoting that you put the information in quotation marks in the text; those quotation marks let your reader know exactly what information comes from another source. In general, you will tend to quote often from primary sources (such as works of literature or major documents that are the focus of your essay). Just because these works are primary sources does not mean you do not have to include citations. All information from sources other than yourself must be cited. In addition to quotations, paraphrased information also receives a citation, but you do not and should not include quotation marks.

There are several different standard formats for citations and bibliographies. Some teachers might also have personal preferences. Ask your professor the way in which you should cite and credit sources in your essay and make certain you follow it. Popular formats currently used in most schools are those that have been developed by the Modern Language Association (MLA) and the American Psychological Association (APA), and are known as the

> Always give credit where credit is due in a clear manner.

MLA and APA formats. You can purchase a handbook for either format that details the specific ways to cite and credit sources.

In general, these standard formats consist of two components: citations within the essay and the list of works cited or bibliography at the conclusion of the essay. Whenever you quote or paraphrase another source, you must include a citation with that sentence or passage that indicates which source it comes from, as well as the location within the source (such as page numbers for books and articles, or line numbers for poems and verse dramas). These citations are usually abbreviations for the whole source, such as the author's last name or a key word in the source's title:

(O'Neill, *Long Day's Journey*, 45)

or

[1] O'Neill, *Long Day's Journey*, p. 45.

This citation in the text corresponds to a listing in the bibliography or works cited section at the end of the essay, where the full publication information for each source is listed:

BIBLIOGRAPHY
O'Neill, Eugene. *Long Day's Journey Into Night*. New Haven: Yale University Press, 1955.

Sample Essay Paragraph with Citations from Other Sources (MLA Format)

The repetition of various images and themes in *Long Day's Journey Into Night* enables O'Neill to reveal past information without resorting to unrealistic methods. In the smaller groupings, characters discuss their past lives a great deal, but it does not seem unnatural or forced because O'Neill takes great pains to tell us that these arguments about the past often take place (Tiusanen 117, Chothia 169-170). As Laurin Porter explains, characters in the play anticipate each other's lines and arguments, an indication of how often these discussions take place (87). For example, Jamie tells Tyrone he "could see that line coming! God, how many thousand times!" (33). Characters often acknowledge the repetitious nature of their arguing, such as when Jamie tells Mary that he and Tyrone have been arguing over "the same old stuff" (40) and when Mary tells the boys, "you've heard me say this a thousand times" (61). O'Neill thereby does more than merely tell us that the family fights about the past constantly; he actually shows them doing it, emphasizing how much the past still dominates the present for them.

Works Cited

(This would appear at the end of the essay that contains the above paragraph; each reference to an outside source in the text corresponds to a listing in the Works Cited.)

Chothia, Jean. *Forging a Language: A Study of the Plays of Eugene O'Neill*. Cambridge: Cambridge University Press, 1979.

O'Neill, Eugene. *Long Day's Journey Into Night*. New Haven: Yale University Press, 1955.

Porter, Laurin. *The Banished Prince: Time, Memory and Ritual in the Late Plays of Eugene O'Neill*. Ann Arbor: UMI Research Press, 1988.

Tiusanen, Timo. "Through the Fog Into the Monologue: *Long Day's Journey Into Night*." in *Eugene O'Neill: A Collection of Criticism*. Ed. Ernest G. Griffin. New York: McGraw-Hill, 1976. 114-129.

Choosing the Correct Type of Citation

Depending on the format you follow for your essay, there are several different kinds of citations, including *in-text/ parenthetical citations*, *footnotes*, and *endnotes*.

In-text/parenthetical citations, as the name indicates, are found within the body of the text, immediately after the sentence or section that has been quoted or paraphrased. They are usually placed within parentheses just before the period. The in-text citation is an abbreviated form of the source; it always corresponds to a more extensive listing in the bibliography at the end of the text. Although they do differ in terms of the specific way in which information is cited, both the MLA and APA formats recommend using in-text citations.

MLA Format In-Text Citation
The fog is the central symbol in Eugene O'Neill's *Long Day's Journey Into Night* (Alberts 42).

When using in-text/parenthetical citations, you include as much information in the parentheses as necessary to clearly indicate to the reader which source in the bibliography the material comes from. For example, if a single author has written several books or articles, you would need to include more information than the author's last name to avoid confusion. In that case, you could include the author's last name and the title. If the title is more than two or three words, you can include one or two key words:

(Alberts, *Symbolism* 42)

At the same time, you don't want the citation to repeat information that is already in the body of the essay. For example, if the body of the essay makes it clear which writer or book the source comes from, you do not need to include that information in the citation:

In Mark Albert's study of O'Neill's writing, *Eugene O'Neill's Flair for Symbolism*, he argues that the fog is the central symbol of *Long Day's Journey Into Night* (42).

Footnotes and endnotes are both more traditional forms of citation. Both are citations not found within the body of the paper. Instead, a footnote will be located at the bottom of the page, and an endnote will be found at the end of the entire paper. Within the text, a raised numeral will follow the passage that has been quoted or paraphrased. That numeral corresponds directly to the footnote or endnote that includes the more detailed information about the source. The notes are numbered consecutively throughout the paper. Generally, the first time you cite another source in a footnote, you include the full publication information for that book. In all other citations from that source that follow, you can use an abbreviated citation, such as the author's last name and the book's title (or key words from the title).

Footnote/Endnote

In the text:
     The fog is the central symbol in Eugene O'Neill's *Long Day's Journey Into Night.*[1]

Bottom of the page or end of text:
[1]Mark Alberts, *Eugene O'Neill's Flair for Symbolism* (New York: Publications Inc.), p. 42.
[2]Alberts, *Flair for Symbolism*, p. 101.

Another type of note you may use is the *content note*. Content notes resemble footnotes or endnotes but they are not citations (they can only be used when in-text citations are already employed). Content notes provide additional information or explanations of what has been discussed in the body of the paper. For example, there might be certain material you wish to include that, while relevant to your essay, would disrupt the flow of the text if included in the body of the paper. Content notes are often used to elaborate upon or evaluate a source, to provide additional background information, or to take issue with a specific critic or researcher and thereby distinguish your own point of view. However, they should be used sparingly; too many content notes can make the paper confusing for the reader and overshadow the power of your own argument.

Content Note

In the text:

The fog is the central symbol in Eugene O'Neill's *Long Day's Journey Into Night* (Alberts 42).[1]

Bottom of the page or end of text:

[1] I agree with Alberts that the fog is the most prominent and prevalent symbol in the play; however, it is also worth noting, as Susan Peters writes in her essay, "More than the Fog," that the fog functions along with other symbols in the play, such as the fog horn, wedding gown, and bottle of liquor, which are dependent upon one another to convey symbolic meaning.

The Bibliography or Works Cited List

All research papers must have a *bibliography*, often called the *works cited* list (a broader definition that refers to listings of both print and nonprint sources), which compiles all the outside sources that are introduced in the paper, giving full publication information for each. All of the parenthetical references and/or footnotes and endnotes must correspond to listings in the works cited.

General Guidelines

You should derive the bibliographic information from the title page or copyright page of the sources (or the cover or index of journals and periodicals). Always cite authors' names and titles exactly as they appear in the source. For example, if the original source uses the author's first initial rather than full name, duplicate this format in the works cited citation.

In general, the works cited list will be alphabetized according to authors' last names. If a source is written by more than one author, it will be alphabetized according to the last name of the first author listed. If there is no author, the work will be alphabetized according to the first significant word in the title. The works cited list should appear on a new page following the conclusion of the paper or the endnotes.

The first line of each citation is flush with the left margin, while subsequent lines in the same citation are indented five spaces. The entire works cited list is double-spaced, both between lines and between citations.

Format for Citations in the Works Cited List

As with the citations, there are specific formats for listing sources in the works cited/bibliography section. The way you list the source depends upon the type of source; there are different ways to list books, essays within anthologies, journal entries, and magazine articles.

The following pages provide general guidelines and list examples of the most common types of bibliography entries so that you can see the different information you must include, depending on the type of source. However, when it comes to citing sources, there are many rules, and exceptions to rules. You should consult your professor and look at a format handbook for more specific guidelines and for how to cite less common types of sources.

> * *Book By a Single Author:*
> Author's Last Name, First Name or Initial. *Title*. City of Publication: Publisher, Year of Publication.

Generally, book titles and major works of literature should be underlined or put in italics.

> Bradley, A.C. *Shakespearean Tragedy*. London: Macmillan, 1904.
> Brustein, Robert. *The Theatre of Revolt: An Approach to Modern Drama*. Boston: Atlantic Monthly Press, 1962.
> O'Neill, Eugene. *Long Day's Journey Into Night*. New Haven: Yale University Press, 1955.

When sources are written by more than one author, list the authors in the same order as they appear on the title page, separating each by a comma and writing "and" before the last name in the list. Reverse only the first author's name.

Magalaner, Marvin, and Richard M. Kain. *Joyce: The Man, the Work, the Reputation*. Westport: Greenwood Press, 1956.

If you are listing more than three authors, you only need to name the first author; use the abbreviation *et al.* to indicate there are additional authors. However, if you prefer, you can list all the authors by name.

Klaus, Carl H., et al. Stages of Drama: Classical to Contemporary Theater. Glenview: Scott, Foresman and Company, 1981.

* *Anthologies/Compilations:*
Editor's Last Name, First Name or Initial, ed. [or comp.] Title. City of Publication: Publisher, Year of Publication.

If you are citing an entire anthology or compilation (and not just a single work from it), list the citation according to the last name of the editor or compiler, using the abbreviation *ed.* or *comp.* following the name.

Bloom, Harold, ed. *Modern Critical Interpretations: Charlotte Bronte's Jane Eyre*. New York: Chelsea House, 1987.
Graham, Don, ed. *Critical Essays on Frank Norris*. Boston: G.K. Hall, 1980.

* *A Work Within an Anthology or Collection:*
Author's Last Name, Author's First Name or Initial.
    "Title of Work Within Anthology." *Title of*
    Anthology. Ed. Editor's Full Name. City of
    Publication: Publisher, Year of Publication.
    Inclusive Pages of Work Within the Anthology.

An article or essay title is normally in quotation marks,
while the title of the anthology will be underlined or in italics.

Eagleton, Terry. "Jane Eyre: A Marxist Study." *Modern*
    Critical Interpretations: Charlotte Bronte's Jane
    Eyre. Ed. Harold Bloom. New York: Chelsea
    House, 1987. 29-45.

If you are citing several works from one anthology or
collection, you do not have to repeat the full publication
information for each. Include a full citation for the entire
collection and use cross-references for the individual works
you wish to cite within it. For the cross-references, list the
editor's last name and the relevant page numbers following
the title of the individual work:

Bloom, Harold, ed. *Modern Critical Interpretations:*
    Charlotte Bronte's Jane Eyre. New York: Chelsea
    House, 1987.
Eagleton, Terry. "Jane Eyre: A Marxist Study." Bloom,
    29-45.

* *An Introduction, Preface, Foreword or Afterword:*
Last Name of Author [of introduction, preface, etc.],
    First Name or Initial. Name of Part of Book Being
    Cited [i.e., Introduction.]. *Title of Complete Work.*
    By Author of Complete Work. City of Publication:
    Publisher, Year of Publication. Inclusive Pages of
    Part Within the Complete Work.

Cite an introduction, preface, foreword, or afterword
according to the author of that specific part. Then identify the
part of the work by name (introduction, preface, etc.), followed by the title and author or editor of the complete work.

Kermode, Frank. Introduction. *The Tragedy of Hamlet,*
    Prince of Denmark. By William Shakespeare. *The*
    Riverside Shakespeare. Ed. G. Blakemore Evans.
    Boston: Houghton Mifflin, 1974. 1135-1140.

* *An Anonymous Title:*
Title. City of Publication: Publisher, Year of Publication.

If the author of a source is anonymous or unknown, cite
the book beginning with the title, and alphabetize it within
the works cited list by the first significant word in the title.

The Owl and the Nightingale. Trans. Brian Stone. New
    York: Penguin, 1971.

* *An Article in a Newspaper:*

Last Name of Author of Article, First Name or Initial.
"Title of Article." *Name of Newspaper* Date Month
Year, edition [if applicable]:page/section numbers.

If it is not clear from the title which city a newspaper comes from, put the city and state in brackets following the name of the newspaper. This is not necessary, however, for national newspapers, such as *USA Today*. If applicable, include the specific edition (morning, evening, late, etc.). Use abbreviations for months. Try to give as specific page numbers as possible, including section numbers or letters as well as pages.

Gussow, Mel. "The Daring Visions of Four New
Young Playwrights." *New York Times* 13 Feb. 1977,
sec. 2:1-13.
Schmitt, Eric. "Army Women Face Bias on Macho Base."
New York Times 2 Aug. 1992, late ed.:28 L.

* An Article in a Magazine:
Last Name of Author of Article, First Name or Initial.
"Title of Article." *Name of Magazine* Date and/or
Month Year: pages.

For weekly or biweekly magazines, include the complete date. For monthly magazines, just include the month (or months) and the year.

Turque, Bill, et al. "The War for the West: Fighting for
the Soul of America's Mythic Land." *Newsweek* 30
Sept. 1991:18-35.

VerMeulen, Michael. "Sam Shepard: Yes, Yes, Yes."
  Esquire Feb. 1980:79-81, 85-86.

* An Article in a Journal:
Last Name of Author of Article, First Name or Initial.
  "Title of Article." *Name of Journal* Volume and/or
  Issue Number (Year):page numbers.

Most scholarly journals are grouped together in bound volumes. For these journals, each issue will have a volume number and an issue number (within the larger volume). If a journal numbers its pages continuously throughout the entire volume, you do not need to include the issue number; the volume number will be sufficient to indicate the source's location. However, if each issue is paginated separately (meaning that each begins with page one), then you need to list both the volume and issue number (separated by a period). Get the volume number from the cover of the journal or the bound volume's spine.

As long as the journal does have a volume number, you never need to give a more specific date than the year. You can ignore days and months, even if they are listed on the cover of the journal. Again, let common sense be your guide; include the information necessary for the reader to locate the source without a problem.

Ceynowa, Andrzej. "The Dramatic Structure of Dutchman."
  Black American Literature Forum 17.1 (1983):15-18.
Hall, Jean. "The Socialized Imagination: Shelley's The
  Cenci and Prometheus Unbound." Studies in
  Romanticism 23 (1984):339-350

Tips for Good Writing

Respect Yourself — and Your Ideas

Your ideas are the most important part of your paper or essay. You should have spent time and effort to develop sophisticated, smart ideas. As you write, you want to work to make those ideas as clear and interesting as possible. After writing your essay's first draft, you should therefore concentrate on your writing style, aiming to convey ideas clearly and in an appropriate and interesting style. This section includes several strategies for helping you communicate your ideas clearly and effectively on paper.

Striving for Clarity

One way in which you can ensure the paper is clearly organized is by focusing each paragraph around a specific point. The body should always be written in paragraphs, not in one long chunk of text. Each paragraph should focus upon a specific point you want to make, and every sentence in that paragraph should relate to that point. Any sentence in the paragraph that doesn't tie into that point should be taken out of the paragraph. It's also a good idea to begin each paragraph with a topic sentence that generally introduces the subject matter or main idea of the paragraph. The topic sentence can also serve as a transition between ideas, demonstrating how the next paragraph builds on, contrasts, or departs from the previous one.

A Well-Structured Paragraph

Despite the carefully contrived way in which O'Neill structures the play in order to present various combinations of characters alone on stage together, he maintains the play's highly realistic frame and maintains the illusion that we are witnessing one day in the life of the family. We see the characters go about their business, and we occasionally see them alone on stage with other characters in the living room, but never in a contrived manner that makes us too aware of the playwright at work. Characters leave the room to do what they normally would on any given day. For example, in the first act, Edmund goes upstairs to get a book, Jamie and Tyrone go outside to work on the hedge, and Mary supervises Bridget in the kitchen. We thereby have the opportunity to see each character alone with the others, but always in an appropriate mode that stays within the play's realistic constraint. In fact, this structuring enhances the play's realism. With many different interactions taking place within the living room, and with so much movement in and out of the room, O'Neill gives the impression that this is a typical day in the life of a real family.

Including transitional words and phrases in certain sentences, particularly topic sentences, particularly helps indicate to your reader how different points are related to one another. There are many transitional words and phrases you can use to connect various sentences and paragraphs, including these:

> To build upon a previous sentence or paragraph: *and, also, additionally, as a result, consequently, further, furthermore, in addition, moreover*
>
> To compare with a previous sentence or paragraph: *similarly, in the same manner, likewise, at the same time, by the same token*
>
> To contrast with a previous sentence or paragraph: *however, but, in contrast, nevertheless, although, yet, on the other hand*
>
> To summarize or draw a conclusion: *therefore, in other words, in short, to sum up, thus*

Common Grammatical Errors

The ideas are the most vital part of any essay; without strong ideas, an essay is not going to be impressive, no matter how well-written it is. However, using correct grammar is also considered an important component of writing essays for school; correct grammar makes it easier for the reader to understand and appreciate your ideas in the first place.

Each sentence and paragraph in the body should flow
smoothly and logically from one to the next.

There are many different grammatical rules, and you
can't possibly memorize them all. However, you don't necessarily have to. You learn to speak without learning the
"rules" of conversation by listening to others; you can also
learn about grammar and language usage by reading. The
more you read, the more you develop an "ear" for correct
grammar. When you write, something will "sound" right
or wrong to you. Try to read more frequently and trust
your "ear" for correct grammar. However, if you have a
serious problem with grammar, you may consider working
with a tutor.

Here is a list of some of the more common errors in
grammar, punctuation and language usage. These are
errors you should particularly watch out for when you are
proofreading your essay.

Homophones

Homophones are words that sound alike but have different spellings and meanings. As they sound similar, they
are extremely easy to confuse in your writing. Even
when you proofread carefully, they can escape your
attention. When you read over your final draft, watch
out for homophones and make certain you have chosen
the correct word.

These are some of the most commonly confused homophones:

its	it's
your	you're
two	too
there	their
whose	who's

Sentence Fragments

A *sentence fragment* is a group of words that does not function as a complete sentence. A complete sentence must consist of an independent clause — a group of words that includes a subject and verb and can stand on its own. The most common type of sentence fragment is one that lacks either a subject or or a verb. You can usually correct a fragment by adding a subject or verb, or join separate fragments by adding a comma.

Fragments:
Ate dinner at home. (no subject)
His next-door neighbor the doctor. (no verb)

Complete Sentences:
Mark ate dinner at home.
His next-door neighbor is a doctor.

When you proofread your essay, make certain each sentence has both a subject and a verb.

Run-on Sentences

Run-on sentences are the opposite of fragments. While a fragment does not contain an independent clause, a run-on sentence strings along one clause or phrase after another, confusing the reader:

> *A Doll's House* is a play by Henrik Ibsen that depicts a middle class marriage where the husband treats the wife, Nora, like a doll but in the end she asserts her independence and she decides to leave him but first she sits him down and tells him the reasons why she is leaving and says she realizes she had been living an illusion with him and had never really done what she wanted.

As you can see in the above sentence, a run-on is very confusing to read; you get lost somewhere in the middle of the sentence and forget what the whole thing is all about. Most run-on sentences can be rewritten as two or three shorter sentences; this makes them easier to read and understand:

> *A Doll's House* is a play by Henrik Ibsen that depicts a middle class marriage. The husband treats the wife, Nora, like a doll. In the end, she asserts her independence and decides to leave him. First she sits him down and tells him the reasons why she is leaving. She says she realizes she has been living an illusion and has never really done what she wanted.

Pronoun-Antecedent Agreement

Pronouns (such as *he, she, him, her, his, hers, they, their, it, its*) take the place of nouns, and the nouns to which they refer are called *antecedents*. Pronouns and antecedents must always agree. That means they must both be either singular or plural.

>   *Incorrect (Pronoun and Antecedent do not agree):*
>   The students took his tests.

>   *Correct (Pronoun and Antecedent are both plural):*
>   The students took their tests.

There are two cases where this grammatical issue particularly becomes a problem: *indefinite pronouns* and *generic nouns.* An indefinite pronoun refers to a nonspecific person or thing (such as *anybody, anyone, everybody, someone*). A generic noun represents a typical member of a group (such as *a doctor, a student, a New Yorker*). Although you might not realize it, both of these kinds of antecedents are followed by singular pronouns. You should either use *he, she,* or *one* as the pronoun, or rewrite the sentence to avoid the problem.

>   *Incorrect:*
>   When everyone has finished their exam, the test is over.
>   A doctor must be considerate of their patients' feelings.

>   *Correct:*
>   When everyone has finished his or her exam, the test is over.
>   A doctor must be considerate of his or her patients' feelings.
>   *or*
>   Doctors must be considerate of their patients' feelings.

Ambiguous References

Broad, nonspecific references, such as *this*, *that*, *which*, and *it*, are ambiguous; it's not always clear to what they refer, which can confuse your reader. You should clearly indicate the person, object, subject, or idea to which these words refer.

> *Ambiguous Phrasing:*
> Hamlet screams at Ophelia and tells her to go to a nunnery. This eventually drives her insane.

> *More Clearly Phrased As:*
> Hamlet screams at Ophelia and tells her to go to a nunnery. This treatment of her eventually drives her insane.

Similarly, when you use pronouns such as *he, she, him, her, his,* or *hers,* you must make certain the reader knows the specific person to whom the pronoun refers.

> *Ambiguous Phrasing:*
> Claudius and Hamlet fight. He kills him.

In the example above, we don't know who kills and who is killed. These sentences can be more clearly phrased this way:

> Claudius and Hamlet fight. Hamlet kills the king.

Dangling Modifiers

Modifiers are words or phrases that describe or elaborate upon some other word or phrase. Dangling modifiers do not logically refer to any word in the sentence and therefore make the sentence incoherent. Be particularly careful when a sentence begins with a modifier; whatever subject follows the modifier must be the one to which the modifier refers.

Incorrect:
Originally performed in 1955, many people still consider *Cat on a Hot Tin Roof* to be Tennessee Williams's greatest play.

In the above sentence, the modifier "originally performed in 1955" refers to the play *"Cat on a Hot Tin Roof,"* and not the "many people." The sentence should therefore be rephrased.

Correct:
Originally performed in 1955, *Cat on a Hot Tin Roof* is still considered by many people to be Tennessee Williams's greatest play.

Split Infinitives

An infinitive form of a verb consists of two parts: the word *to* plus the verb. An infinitive is "split" when another word comes between the two parts. Although certain constructions featuring split infinitives have come to be accepted, they generally sound awkward and disrupt the flow of a sentence. You should generally avoid them.

Split Infinitive:
My parents taught me to slowly eat.

Intact:
My parents taught me to eat slowly.

Sentences Ending in Prepositions

Prepositions are certain words, usually appearing at the beginning of a phrase, that are used to describe or elaborate on some other word in the sentence.

There are a limited number of prepositions in English. The most common ones include: *about, above, across, after, against, along, among, around, as, at, before, behind, below, beside, between, but, by, concerning, despite, during, except, for, from, in, into, like, near, next, of, off, on, onto, out, over, regarding, respecting, since, than, through, throughout, to, toward, under, underneath, unlike, until, unto, up, upon, with, without.*

It is generally considered poor grammar to end a sentence with a preposition. If a sentence ends with preposition, you should rephrase it.

Incorrect:
He couldn't get around the couple so he walked between.
She didn't understand what the remark referred to.

Correct:

He couldn't get around the couple so he walked between them.

She didn't understand to what the remark referred.

Say It with Style

Every piece of writing has its own distinctive style. The style reflects the manner in which something is written and depends on such factors as the choice of words, the sentence patterns, and the way in which ideas are introduced. An essay's style indicates the writer's attitude toward the material, and signals to the reader how to respond. For example, the style can indicate if a work is serious, sarcastic, humorous, or silly.

When you are writing an academic essay or term paper, you generally want to use a sophisticated, intelligent style. In so doing, you convey to the reader your expertise in the subject area and your professional attitude toward it.

In trying to create this impression, you should avoid being too chatty or conversational. You don't want to use slang or casual expressions; instead, you should use serious and intelligent vocabulary. You also want to write sentences that are more varied and complex in structure than "See Dick run." At the same time, you don't want to overdo it. If you try too hard to write in a sophisticated manner, you might make the essay too confusing for the reader.

Too Conversational:

Long Day's Journey Into Night is such a bummer to read. The Tyrone family is really, really having a lousy time trying to communicate. They should really get with it and start dealing with stuff.

Too Wordy and Overwritten:

Eugene O'Neill's magnum opus, *Long Day's Journey Into Night*, bears upon the reader with the weight of its tragic philosophizing of the historicity of this particular familial unit. The Tyrones, as they are deemed in the work, are prey to such overpowering dramatic forces as fate, the gods, their genes, and the distinctive, saturnine environmental setting, which is incidentally an obvious homage to the great naturalist works of Zola and Strindberg. These four lost souls need to penetrate the steel-like veneer of familial normalcy and at last examine their flaws, failings, and feelings.

Sophisticated Yet Direct Style:

Long Day's Journey Into Night undoubtedly has a powerful effect upon any contemporary reader. The Tyrones are clearly a dysfunctional family grappling, like so many families, with issues of communication. One senses that if the family would cease dredging up past events, they could at last address their present problems and make positive changes for the future.

The last paragraph makes an intelligent comment about the play and weaves in some sophisticated vocabulary. However, it remains a direct, easy-to-read statement that will not confuse the reader.

When using a thesaurus, you need to be careful about which synonym you choose. Although the synonyms have the same basic meaning, there are sometimes slight differences. Certain words are also more appropriate for a particular context. Additionally, some of the synonyms might be old-fashioned words not frequently used. If you include them in your essay, these words will stand out and disrupt the flow of your argument.

Write with style, but make certain it is a style appropriate for an essay. Let your writing indicate intelligence and sophistication, without being too highbrow or convoluted.

Variety Is the Spice of Writing

If you read a paragraph or passage that uses the same words over and over it can become quite boring and tedious. To make an essay more interesting for your reader, you should try to vary your choice of words as much as possible. You particularly want to include sophisticated vocabulary that indicates your intelligence and expertise.

To help increase the variety of your word choices, you can use a thesaurus — a special dictionary that compiles synonyms of words. Synonyms are words that essentially have the same meaning. Sometimes a thesaurus will also list antonyms, which are words with the opposite meaning.

There are several types of thesauruses on the market, and some are much easier to use than others. Look for a thesaurus

Only choose synonyms with which you are familiar and comfortable using in your writing. If necessary, you can look up some of the suggested synonyms in a dictionary in order to see the exact definition and appropriate context.

that is organized in dictionary form, listing words in alphabetical order followed by their many synonyms and antonyms. Using this kind of thesaurus is as easy as looking up a definition in a dictionary; you simply look for the word for which you want to find alternatives, and you'll see all of the synonyms listed beside it. With a thesaurus that is not organized in dictionary form, you'll instead find cross-listings and cross-references. That means that when you look for a particular word, you won't necessarily find synonyms for it; instead, you'll be referred to another word or part of a word, where you will then find a more extensive listing of synonyms.

When you edit your paper, look for any words that are repeated many times, especially within the same paragraph. You can then look up the words in the thesaurus and select alternatives.

For example, the following passage repeats variations on the same word:

> *Long Day's Journey Into Night* illustrates the many <u>tensions</u> in the Tyrone family. The family members' relationships are fraught with <u>tension</u>. Each conversation between family members is also <u>tense</u>.

With the help of a thesaurus, you can easily find synonyms that make the passage more varied and interesting:

> *Long Day's Journey Into Night* illustrates the many <u>tensions</u> in the Tyrone family. The family members' relationships are fraught with <u>strain and anxiety</u>. Each conversation between family members is <u>uneasy</u>.

Word Power

As we noted, based on the words you use and the way you use them, the reader is going to get an impression of you in terms of your intelligence and sophistication. For that reason, you want to be careful to use words that convey your intelligence as well as the seriousness with which you approach your work. In general, while you are in school, it's a good idea to work on improving your vocabulary. Having a good vocabulary will help improve your reading and study skills in general. It can also help improve the overall tone and style of your essay. Whenever you read, get in the habit of looking up words you don't understand; you might even keep a list of new words you learn. As you become comfortable with these more sophisticated words, you can begin to put them into your writing. Just be careful when you use a word in your essay that you are using it properly.

To help get you started, here is a list of vocabulary words you can use in your writing and conversation that are guaranteed to make you sound more intelligent. For each word, you'll find a concise definition and an example of the word used in a sentence. After you've mastered these words, be on the lookout in your reading for additional vocabulary words you can learn and put into use. The key to learning new words is using them frequently.

evince— to display clearly, show or reveal
A detailed study of these two plays will *evince* many similarities between them.

formulate— to put into a set statement or expression, to devise (as in a policy or plan)
The novel's theme is *formulated* in the final chapter.

fortuitous— lucky, happening by chance, accidental
It was certainly *fortuitous* that they ran into each other in London.

germane— relevant, appropriate to, fitting
A discussion of bone structure is certainly *germane* to our study of anatomy.

hegemony— those persons or institutions in power over others
The church was a *hegemonic* institution in the Middle Ages.

heinous— shockingly evil and hateful
Richard III is the most *heinous* of Shakespeare's villains.

illuminate— to make clear, shed light on
This paper will *illuminate* the specific connections between the author's life and work.

ingenuous— showing innocent and child-like simplicity and candor; noble and honest, trusting
She is so *ingenuous*, she will trust just about anyone.

juxtapose— to place side by side for the sake of comparison
If we *juxtapose* a painting by Van Gogh with one by Matisse, their similar use of color becomes clear.

manifest— to make evident or certain by showing or displaying
His concern for the underprivileged has been made *manifest* many times by his extensive volunteer work.

ontological— relating to the nature of existence and our knowledge of it
Her writings have taken an *ontological* twist now that she has begun to discuss more personal issues.

perspicacity— acute mental power; shrewdness
Your adept performance in that oral examination demonstrated your *perspicacity*.

plethora— an abundance or excess
To prove my point, I will raise a *plethora* of sources and pieces of evidence.

praxis— customary action or practice
It is usually easier to understand something in *praxis* rather than theory.

preponderance— a majority; a superiority in power, importance, number, or strength

In the election, she has a *preponderance* of devoted followers.

prevalent— widespread; generally accepted, seen or favored

Signs that the economy is not doing well are certainly *prevalent*.

Do It Your Way

Developing your own style as a writer takes time. You need to discover a voice in which you are comfortable expressing yourself that also conveys a particular impression to your intended audience. At first, strive primarily for clarity; work at conveying your ideas as clearly and directly as possible so that the reader can learn and understand what you have to say. The more you read and write over time, the more you'll gain a sense of various writing styles — and begin to develop your own.

Editing, Proofreading, and Preparing the Final Paper

Editing for Length

When you are finished revising your essay several times and are generally satisfied with it, check to be sure you have met the page requirements set by your teacher. Remember, choosing the right topic from the start is the best way to ensure your essay will turn out to be the appropriate length. However, once you've gotten started writing, you may find your essay comes out a bit longer or shorter than you intended. If your essay is only a half a page or so longer or shorter, then most professors will still accept it. However, if it is off by more than half a page, then you need to make adjustments.

If the essay is too long, read through it looking specifically for sentences and paragraphs that don't contribute a significant point to the essay. Examine all the points you've made to support the thesis, pick out whichever one is weakest and cut out that section of the paper. You can also look for any sections of the paper that needlessly summarize or repeat points that are already quite clear for the reader. Just be certain whenever you make large cuts that you reread the entire essay to see that it still flows smoothly and makes sense.

If the essay is too short, then reread the entire piece looking for any sections that can be developed in more detail. Once again, ask yourself what questions a reader might have while reading the essay that you can answer within the text. You also might try to think up additional examples or illustrations you can add to the paper to support major points in more detail. As a last resort, you can look for additional quotations from outside sources you can integrate into the paper as a way of making it longer. Just make certain you discuss the quotations you include; if you just sprinkle them throughout the essay, it will be obvious to the professor that you are merely padding the essay with unnecessary material.

Proofreading Tips

When you have a final version of your essay at the right length, it's time to proofread it. You want your final essay to be flawless, without any mistakes or incorrect information. Turning in an essay without carefully proofreading makes a very poor impression on a teacher. It indicates that you don't take your work all that seriously. Even if the ideas within the essay are good, not taking the time to proofread can lower your grade significantly. Be sure to take the time to proofread, and do it extremely carefully.

Throughout the entire process of revising and redrafting the essay, you can always watch out for and correct any errors. However, you don't have to make that your primary concern until the final proofread. By not worrying about grammar, punctuation, and spelling until the end, you are free on previous drafts to focus on expressing your ideas in a clear, organized manner. You should also take this time to double-check all of your citations from outside sources. Make certain you have quoted material exactly, that all quoted and paraphrased material is cited clearly, and that you have used the proper format.

When you are ready to proofread, try to use a clean copy of the essay. This is easy if you are working on a computer, as you can simply print out a clean copy. Find a location to read where there are absolutely no distractions. Sit down with the essay and begin to read. It is extremely important that the entire time you read you keep foremost in mind that you are trying to locate errors. If you forget this and get caught up in the essay, you will continue overlooking mistakes. Read slowly and methodically, concentrating on each word and sentence. It is extremely helpful to read the essay out loud, so that you can hear each word. If you don't wish to do this, you can simply mouth the words silently.

Some people recommend reading the essay backward as a means of proofreading. By reading backward, you are not distracted by the writing itself and instead focus on individual words. While this is an effective way to spot spelling errors, it does not necessarily enable you to identify errors of grammar and punctuation, where you need to read the entire sentence as it is written on the page. You may consider doing both — a "normal" reading and a "backward" reading.

If you are working on a computer, don't depend on the spell-check to catch all the mistakes. The spell-check program is indeed helpful and can correct many errors. However, it won't catch everything. For one thing, the spell-check will not catch homophones — words that sound the same but are spelled differently and have different meanings. If you use a homophone in place of the correct word, the spell-check won't detect the error and will simply skip over it. You should always proofread at least once after you've spell-checked your essay.

While proofreading, sit with a dictionary at hand. Get in the habit of looking up the definition of any words in the essay you don't frequently use in conversation. In the process of writing and attempting to sound sophisticated, it is easy to use a word you think means one thing when it actually means something quite different. You should therefore double-check definitions of words in the dictionary to make certain you've used them correctly.

Additionally, become aware of particular spelling or grammatical errors you are prone to make; whenever you get back an essay from a teacher, read it over to identify any patterns of errors. When you go to proofread future essays, be sure to look specifically for those mistakes you tend to make.

Proofreading is a tedious process, but it is an important one. Remember, your writing is a reflection of you. A carefully proofread paper indicates a professional and serious attitude to the reader. And when the reader is your teacher, isn't that the impression you want to make?

A PROOFREADING CHECKLIST

Be certain you particularly check these elements in your final proofreading session:

- Spelling errors
- Mixed up homophones (words that sound the same but are spelled differently)
- Incorrect word usage
- Sentence fragments
- Run-on sentences
- Citation format
- Ambiguous references and pronouns (especially *it, that, this, these,* and *those*)
- Pronoun-antecedent agreement
- Comma usage
- Quotation marks (make certain all quotations have quotation marks at the beginning and end of the quoted section)
- Apostrophes used correctly (especially with possessive nouns and contractions)
- Capitalization
- Consistent verb tense

Remember to be on the lookout for those specific mistakes you tend to make often.

Here's a list of frequently misspelled words. Watch for them in your writing and double-check to see if they are correct.

absence	emphasize
accessible	exaggerate
accommodate	exercise
acquaintance	existence
achieve	exorcise
across	guarantee
appearance	half/halves
athlete	indefinitely
benefited/benefiting	independent
bureaucracy	indispensable
business	insistent
changeable	interpret
commitment	judgment
committed	knowledge
conscience	loneliness
definitely	medicine
difference/different	noticeable
embarrass	occasionally

(continued)

occur/occurred/occurrence	self/selves
offer/offered/offering	separate
omit/omitted	significance
parallel	sophomore
peace/peaceable	succeed/successful
perseverance	terrific
preference/preferred	their
prevalence	tragedy
privilege	transfer/transferred
pursue	undoubtedly
refer/referred/referring	unnecessary
repetition	vacuum
rhythm	worshipped
seize	

Dazed and Confused

The following list contains words or expressions that are frequently confused or misused. Most of them are homophones, words that sound the same but are spelled differently and therefore have different meanings. Get to know the words on this list so you can watch out for them in your writing and double-check to make certain you use them correctly.

affect/effect

affect — used as a verb meaning to influence or to change
(The noise *affects* my ability to think.)

effect — used as a noun, meaning the result of
something
(The noise produces a negative *effect* on my work.)

capital/capitol

capital — the seat of government (such as the city that
is the state capital)

capitol — the building in which a governing body meets
(as in the Capitol Building in Washington D.C.)

center on/revolve around

It is incorrect to say that something centers *around* or
revolves *on* a subject;

something can only center *on* or revolve *around* a subject.

its/it's

its — a possessive; refers to what "it" owns

it's — a contraction of "it is"
(*It's* fun to watch the dog fetch *its* toys.)

media/medium

medium — a singular form of the word media referring
to a single type of mass communication such as
radio or television

media — a plural form of the word medium that refers
to several types of communication or to mass communication in general.
(Television is a *medium* that is far more influential
and important than the other *media*.)

principle/principal
principle — a rule or law; a fact of nature
principal — a person in authority, such as the head of a
school
(remember, the princi*pal* is your *pal*).

quote/quotation
quote — used as a verb meaning to repeat something
from another source
quotation — used as a noun meaning the reference that
is repeated from another source
(He proceeded to *quote* from the passage, and the
quotation was quite long.)

stationary/stationery
stationary — standing still
stationery — materials used for writing and typing
(The clerk was *stationary* behind the counter of
stationery.)

than/then

than — used when comparing

then — used in reference to time; the next in order
    or time
    (Let's eat lunch and *then* go to the movies rather
    than the other way around.)

their/there

their — a possessive; refers to something they own

there — refers to location
    (*Their* car is over *there* in that parking lot.)

your/you're

your — a possessive; refers to something you own

you're — a contraction of "you are"
    (*You're* going to be late to pick up *your* car.)

Identifying Your Essay

You should always put a title on your essay, as well as your name, the course name and number, the professor's name, and the date. You can either do this on the first page of the essay or on a separate title page. Ask your professor if he or she has a preference.

If you are putting this information on the first page of the essay, you should go down about one inch and type the following information against the left margin, double-spaced:

Your Name

The Professor's Name

The Course Number and Name

The Date

Then skip another two lines and center the title of the essay above the first paragraph. Do not underline the title or put it in quotation marks.

If you are using a separate title page, all information should be centered on the page. Put your title about one-third of the way down the page. Skip two lines and write the word "By" followed by your name. Below your name, write the course name and number, your instructor's name and the date; skip lines between each piece of information and center each line on the page.

Students often fail to put titles on their essays, but the title is an important component. First and foremost, the title indicates the general topic of the essay. More importantly, like the first paragraph, the title can give the reader a first impression of the writer. Try to conceive of a title that conveys information about the essay but is also intelligent and witty.

One effective strategy for conceiving a title is to use a title and subtitle, separated by a colon. The title should be a short phrase or quotation; the subtitle that follows it should be a longer sentence that explains the essay's topic in more detail:

Open for Business: The Portrayal of Commerce and Economics in the First Scene of Shakespeare's *Merchant of Venice*

"I'll Talk About Anything I Want to George": Vying for Control of Conversation in Edward Albee's *Who's Afraid of Virginia Woolf?*

When writing titles, remember:

- Capitalize the first and last word.
- Capitalize all words in the title except for articles, prepositions, and conjunctions.
- Never put the entire title in quotation marks. However, if there is a quoted phrase *within* the title, you should put that phrase in quotation marks.
- Never underline the entire title. However, if you mention the title of a major work *within* the title of your essay, you should underline the name of the work, or if you are using a word processor, put it in italics.
- Never follow the title with a period.

Meeting the Deadline

It's extremely important that you turn in your essay by the required due date. That means you should leave yourself plenty of time to do all of the research and writing. It also means typing up or printing out the final version at least a day before the essay is due. If you wait until the last minute to prepare the final copy, you risk not being able to get it in on time. Your typewriter or computer or printer might malfunction and then you'll be in trouble. Most teachers are not particularly sympathetic to these excuses for late papers. Plan on finishing your essay a day ahead to make certain you have time to deal with any last-minute problems.

If for some reason you need an extension — because of illness or some other kind of personal crisis that prevents you from finishing on time — go see the professor privately to discuss it. Do not raise the issue during class time; go to see the professor before or after class, or during office hours.

The Final Copy

You've worked hard on your paper, and it deserves to be read. So make sure your reader can read it. Always type the final version of your paper and try to do it as neatly as possible. Don't hand in a paper covered with correction fluid, erasure marks, and pencil scrawling. Neatness always counts and makes a good impression; your instructor will recognize the care you've put into your paper and treat it with more respect. Again, this will be much easier to do if you've been working on a computer; then you merely need to print out the final version.

Term papers should be double-spaced throughout. Always use white paper measuring 8 1/2 x 11 inches. Leave a one-inch margin on the top and bottom of the pages, as well as on the right and left sides. Begin each paragraph by indenting five spaces.

Number the pages consecutively throughout the paper. Place page numbers one-half inch down from the top, in the upper-right-hand corner. Put your last name before each page number in case the pages somehow become separated. Staple or clip the pages together so that they stay together. Don't ever fold over the corners of the pages to keep them together; it makes the essay look sloppy and doesn't really work.

Most important: Always keep a copy of your paper! You never know what might happen to the original. A teacher might accidentally lose it or something could happen on your way to class to turn it in. Cover yourself by having an extra copy at home you can turn in on short notice.

Put Your Best Foot Forward

Your writing is one of the most direct forms of communication between you and your teacher. What your teacher sees in your writing contributes significantly to the impression he or she has of you. An essay that is sloppy and unfocused, filled with typos and grammatical errors, paints a portrait of a student who doesn't care very much about what he or she has turned in. However, an essay that is neat, well-organized, filled with interesting and original ideas, and carefully proofread indicates a student who takes pride in his or her work. You can guess which student will get a higher grade on the essay — and for class participation. Remember, your essay tells the teacher a lot more about you than just your ideas about a particular subject.

FINAL CHECKLIST

Before turning in an essay, run down the following list of questions. If you make certain to do everything on this list, you are more likely to turn in a quality piece of writing.

❏ Are my topic, thesis statement, and general approach clear to the reader?

❏ Have I proven my thesis statement beyond the shadow of a doubt?

❏ Have I made my argument fully and persuasively?

❏ Does every paragraph in the essay clearly relate to the thesis statement?

❏ Does every paragraph center on a single point that is clear to the reader?

❏ Do paragraphs and sentences flow together? Have I included transitions that connect sentences and paragraphs together?

❏ Have I supplied all of the information a reader needs to understand all of my points? Have I anticipated any questions a reader might have and included the answers within the essay?

❏ Have I cut out any excess words, sentences, or paragraphs that don't contribute anything substantial to the paper?

❏ Have I varied my word choices?

❏ Have I altered my sentence patterns?

❏ Have I used all of the words correctly and in the right context?

❏ Have I proofread for grammar, spelling, and punctuation errors?

❏ Have I cited all quoted and paraphrased sections? Have I used the proper citation format? Have I included a bibliography written in the proper format?

❏ Have I typed up a clean, final copy? Is it double-spaced and stapled together? Does each page have a page number and my name? Have I included a title, my name, the course, and the date on the first page of the essay or on a title page?

❏ Have I made an extra copy of the essay to keep?

Index

The Everything Study Book
Steven Frank, ISBN: 1-55850-615-2, $12.00, 276 pages
Reference, Trade paperback

The Everything Study Book presents a totally comprehensive program focused on sharpening your study skills. Whether you simply lack motivation, or your term papers aren't as exciting as you'd like them to be, the proven techniques featured here will put you on track to getting better grades. Author and College instructor Steven Frank has developed step-by-step strategies that will pave the way to success—and boost you confidence!

The Everything College Survival Book
Jason Rich, ISBN: 1-55850-720-5, $12.00, 304 pages
Reference, Trade paperback

This books covers every major issue an incoming freshman should know about the college experience. Roommates, Financial Aid, Fraternities, and Sororities. Studying for exams. It's all here. This book is designed to make the transition into college as smooth as possible.